Paperless FOR LAWYERS

SHEILA M. BLACKFORD AND DONNA S. M. NEFF

ABA LAW
PRACTICE
DIVISION
The Business of Practicing Law

Commitment to Quality: The Law Practice Division is committed to quality in our publications. Our authors are experienced practitioners in their fields. Prior to publication, the contents of all our books are rigorously reviewed by experts to ensure the highest quality product and presentation. Because we are committed to serving our readers' needs, we welcome your feedback on how we can improve future editions of this book.

Cover design by RIPE Creative, Inc.

Library of Congress Cataloging-in-Publication Data

Blackford, Sheila M., author.
  Paperless in one hour for lawyers / by Sheila M. Blackford and Donna S.M. Neff.
    pages cm
  Includes index.
  ISBN 978-1-61438-524-0
  1. Law offices--United States. 2. Law offices--United States--Automation. 3. Paperwork (Office practice)--United States--Automation. 4. Electronic records--United States. I. Neff, Donna S. M. (Donna Sharon Margaret), 1945- author. II. American Bar Association. Law Practice Management Division. III. Title.
  KF318.B53 2014
  651.5'902434--dc23

                                                                                      2013045199

Contents

Lesson 7 Fine-Tune Your System: Focus on the Details **63**

Lesson 8 Apps for the Paperless Lawyer **79**

About the Authors

Sheila M. Blackford

Oregon State Bar Professional Liability Fund, Tigard, Oregon

Sheila Blackford received her B.A. from Mills College and her J.D. with Tax Law Concentration from McGeorge School of Law. A member of the Oregon State Bar since 2000, she is active with the American Bar Association Law Practice Division, where she is Editor-in-Chief of *Law Practice* magazine and Chair of the *Law Practice* Magazine Editorial Board (2011-present), a member of the Section Council (2010-present), State and Local Bar Outreach Committee (2008-present), and Ethics Committee (2011-present). She also served as a member of the track advisory board for ABA TECHSHOW (2007, 2008, 2009, 2012).

Ms. Blackford has been a Practice Management Advisor for the Oregon State Bar Professional Liability Fund since 2005. She is a member of the Adjunct Faculty at University of Oregon School of Law, teaching *Law Practice Management*. A former sole practitioner, she provides confidential practice management assistance to Oregon attorneys to reduce their risk of malpractice claims and ethics complaints. In addition to her legal experience, she has over 10 years of teaching and marketing experience.

She is a frequent speaker about practice management for law-related organizations, including the Professional Liability Fund, the Oregon State Bar, the American Bar Association, and the Law Society of Upper Canada. She is a contributing author to the *Fee Agreement Compendium* published by the OSB and to the PLF law practice management handbooks. Her articles frequently appear in legal publications, including the *Oregon State Bar Bulletin, In Brief, Law Practice Magazine, Law Practice TODAY,* and *LTN Law Technology News.* In between articles, she writes the Just Oregon Lawyers blog and tweets technology and practice management tips on Twitter.

Donna S.M. Neff, JD, TEP, CS
Neff Law Office Professional Corporation, Ottawa, ON

Donna is a solo attorney with a thriving estates and trusts practice in Ottawa, Canada. She is Certified Specialist (Estates and Trusts Law) by the Law Society. Donna has a keen interest in legal technology having worked for many years as a project management consultant in the high tech industry prior to becoming a lawyer. She attended ABA TECHSHOW for the first time in 2006 and has attended annually ever since. She has implemented many of the strategies and tools that she has learned about at ABA TECHSHOW. Donna was one of the early adopters of the paperless office. Her law firm's website won a national award in the solo/small firm category. She speaks frequently on topics related to her area of practice and speaks to attorneys as she enthusiastically shares her experience in going paperless and how she uses technology to enhance her estates practice and improve client service. Donna joined the ABA TECHSHOW Planning Board in 2010. She is working on her second practice-related book, which provides stories and practical solutions to issues facing families dealing with aging parents. Donna uses both PC (Windows 7) and Apple (iPad, iPhone) tech products and delights in sharing what she learns and applies in her law practice.

Dedication

I dedicate this writing effort to Eric Blackford, my husband, and Michele LaMerrill, my daughter, for their encouragement throughout this process. I thank the following people without whom there would be no book: Donna Neff for her great enthusiasm for and knowledge of this topic; Dan Siegel, Allison Shields, and Tom Mighell for their invaluable editing advice; and Lindsay Dawson at Law Practice Division's Book Publishing for making good LP books appear on bookshelves seemingly without effort.

Introduction

Getting Started

Raise your hand if you are drowning in paper.

As members of the legal community, we generate paper and attract even more. If you're holding this book, either you wonder whether going paperless is a good idea or you already know it's a good idea but are wondering how to do it.

The world is becoming less paper-dependent, but we still do not profess to be completely paper-free. Donna's law office has developed and implemented procedures that allow her firm to do the same jobs with much less paper, and when a client matter is closed, its contents are entirely in digital form. In this book, we'll discuss some strategies to help you do the same in your firm.

The Benefits of Going Paperless

A review of the benefits may help you answer the "What's in it for me?" question and clarify the goals you hope to achieve by moving to a less paper-dependent environment.

Here are some of the many benefits of going paperless:

1. Reduced costs for storing and printing due to the reduced need to store paper files and the limited need for printing

2. Greater efficiency and productivity resulting from improved document management

3. Access to the firm's documents quickly and easily from anywhere with an Internet connection

4. The ability to take an entire file to court without having to lug boxes of paper

5. Less time spent locating and retrieving documents, whether current or archived

6. Greater access to information about a specific document's history of authorship, readership, or modification

7. The ability to control levels of permission for access to each document

8. Improved security: it is more difficult to copy or alter a properly secured electronic document than a paper one

9. The option to decrease office space: with electronic document management, employees can work remotely, and a coordinated work-from-home system means two or more employees can share the same workspace

10. A higher level of client service at low cost

11. Easier compliance with courts, land title offices, and other organizations and tribunals that increasingly expect electronic filings

12. A reduction in the firm's environmental impact both now, as a result of using less paper, and in the future, because of the reduced need for storage space.

The many advantages described previously translate into increased efficiency, better document security, improved client satisfaction, and savings of time and money. These advantages, however, also have an unquantifiable benefit: peace of mind. The sum total of this peace of mind is priceless.

The Consequences of Too Much Paper

The Cost of Lost Productivity

Most law firms generate and accumulate a large amount of paper. It shouldn't come as a surprise that there is an enormous loss of productivity when you spend even fifteen minutes a day searching for a specific document. If your billable rate is $200 an hour, the cost of fifteen minutes of unproductive time is $50 a day, which translates into $250 a week, or $13,000 a year. And if others join you in the search, there is an additional cost for their loss of time as well.

The Cost of Paper Storage

The cost of overhead increases when you need a place to store all that paper. Lateral files and vertical files have two things in common: they are quickly filled, and they take up room in our offices. But office space isn't the only cost, because on-site capabilities are quickly maxed out. Proper storage of paper files requires a secure environment where humidity and moisture is controlled.

Sheila recently talked with an Oregon lawyer who discovered that all the firm's files were covered with mold after two years in a storage facility that was not humidity-controlled. Of course, the cost to re-create a paper file rendered useless from damage is far more than the cost of humidity-controlled storage.

But the expense of keeping closed client files in off-site storage grows exponentially as you continue to close files that need to be maintained for several years to comply with ethical rules and regulations. Your malpractice insurer will likely recommend keeping closed client files for the duration of any statute of ultimate repose for a claim of legal malpractice, frequently ten years from the date the matter is closed. And if you are a criminal defense lawyer, you might need to hold the file of an incarcerated client for a period that may be longer than your lifetime.

The cost of a ten-by-fifteen-foot storage unit is approximately $175 a month in Los Angeles, $270 in Chicago, $250 in Toronto, and $370 in New York. As your storage needs increase, so does the space required, and so does the price. Plus, there's always inflation, and the cost of transferring your files from one vendor to another may well be prohibitive.

On top of the financial expense, it is time-consuming to catalog and prepare paper files for storage and retrieval. As frustrating as it is to search for a client file in your office, trying to find it in storage can be much worse.

The Cost of Digital Docs

In contrast to the space needed to keep paper files, one portable hard drive with a storage capacity of one terabyte can hold all of your client files and much more. One terabyte is one trillion bytes, or one thousand gigabytes. These are huge numbers for storing digital text, which takes up little room compared with audio, images, or video. For example, assuming a five-page document is one hundred kilobytes, a 5.4 million–page document would be one terabyte. For all this storage, one- and even two-terabyte hard drives are available for less than $200. In short, going paperless is the economical and green alternative to filling expensive office space with filing cabinets.

Who Should Read This Book?

This book is for the busy solo or small-firm lawyer who may not have IT support and doesn't have time to read a lot of books, blogs, and articles to get answers about going paperless. This book is also for the lawyer in a bigger firm who wants to do a quick study about going paperless to sell the idea to the rest of the firm and for the managing lawyer or law firm administrator who wants to get background information before putting together a plan for firm-wide rollout.

The two of us are eager to let others know what we've learned about going paperless. Although we share the same enthusiasm and vision, we have arrived at this point through different experiences after first becoming inspired at seminars describing the benefits of a paperless law practice. Sheila encourages lawyers in Oregon to go paperless; Donna runs a paperless, thriving trust and estates practice in Ottawa.

You are busy. We get that. We promise you can read this book in about one hour. Each lesson will be quick and easy to digest, with lots of helpful lists, charts, and screenshots to show you how we've done it and provide tips and tricks to encourage you along the road to going paperless.

Road Map for the Journey

Getting commitment from your team is the first step in embarking on the paperless journey (we will discuss this in-depth in Lesson 6). To prepare for this step, you must have an understanding of the nuts and bolts of the paperless environment.

The Agenda

- Lesson 1: Define Goals and Analyze Workflows
- Lesson 2: Hardware: What You Need
- Lesson 3: Software Applications: What You Need
  - The PDF Format: A Primer
  - Document Management Software
  - A Do-It-Yourself Model of Document Management
- Lesson 4: Establish a Paperless Protocol and Improve Business Practices
- Lesson 5: Take a Closer Look at Cloud-Based Storage
- Lesson 6: How to Get Commitment from Your Team and Buy-in from All Stakeholders
- Lesson 7: Fine-Tune Your System and Focus on the Details
- Lesson 8: Apps for Paperless Lawyers
- Lesson 9: Ethical Considerations
- Conclusion: What Lies Ahead
- Resources
- Appendix: File Naming

Define Goals and Analyze Current Workflows

Going paperless is much easier with some upfront planning and initial groundwork.

First, you need to define and prioritize the specific goals you hope to achieve. Of course you want to reduce your reliance on paper. But going paperless offers many other benefits, as you saw in the introduction. Decide which of these are most important for your office and begin there. Second, analyze how your firm does things now. How does a paper document travel through your office? Which team members are responsible for what steps? These and other questions will help you clarify your current workflows.

Identifying goals and analyzing workflows will help you determine what needs a complete overhaul and what simply needs to be tweaked to ensure a successful transition to going paperless.

Define Your Goals

Goals should be specific and measurable. What are your goals for going paperless? What exactly do you need to do to succeed, and how will you know when you are ready to proudly wear a "We've gone paperless" t-shirt?

Going paperless means different things to different people. Decide, with your team, what going paperless will mean for your firm:

- fewer paper documents or none at all?
- storage needs reduced or eliminated?
- some or all employees could work from home?
- all of the above?

Brainstorm with your entire staff, or your firm's practice group or department, to determine the specific results to be achieved. Here are a few questions to start the discussion:

- What is motivating us to consider going paperless?
- Is there a problem we are trying to solve?
- What part of going paperless excites us most?

Once you have your goals itemized, don't stop there. Prioritize them according to their importance to the team as a whole and their positive effect on the bottom line. Refer to the goals throughout the process of developing your paperless office to ensure they will be met. When you can put a check mark beside each goal, you will know you have "gone paperless."

Donna's initial goal in considering the paperless route was a practical one. Her firm was quickly outgrowing its in-house physical storage capacity. She wasn't keen on paying for additional storage outside the office. Going paperless offered an answer.

And if saving storage costs wasn't enough, Donna soon realized that going paperless could be the answer to her question, "How can a solo lawyer satisfy her love of travel and keep the office going?" The prospect of increased mobility got her globe-trotting heart all aflutter. She was sold. After she spent a month traveling through South America, all the while continuing to run her practice, Donna proudly donned her t-shirt because she knew her firm had successfully gone paperless. Subsequent lengthy trips have also been possible, all because she took her office paperless. Even if all you want is to be able to work from home without having to lug a heavy briefcase with you each night, going paperless is the answer.

Analyze Your Current Workflows

Once you have a clear, defined sense of what you hope to achieve at the end of your paperless adventure, it's time to determine how to efficiently and effectively get to where you want to go.

Review and analyze your current processes and workflows. Be critical of how you do things. Look for every opportunity to improve. You must determine which areas need improvement and which processes are not as efficient as they could be.

Involve your entire team in this exercise. Your staff works with the firm's documents daily and will have valuable insights into what will work and what won't. Encourage everyone to share ideas openly and offer suggestions for improvement.

To get started, explore these questions:
- How does the firm organize paper documents?
- How does the firm organize electronic documents?
- Do these systems work well?
- If not, what would make them better as we go paperless?

- In what ways could paper be reduced?

Look at the paper trail in your office. How do documents flow, from arrival to archiving or destruction? Consider the following for every physical and electronic document:

- How does it arrive?
- Who touches it first?
- Where does it go next?
- How is it saved?
- Where is it saved?
- Is it saved in more than one location?
- Is anyone given a copy?
- How is it retrieved?

One of the biggest benefits of going paperless is the streamlining of routine processes for handling paper. Consider the following example of the monthly bank statement at Donna's firm (see Figure 1.1). In the traditional paper-based law office, the statement arrived in the mail and was handled by various staff members.

Figure 1.1 Traditional Bank Statement

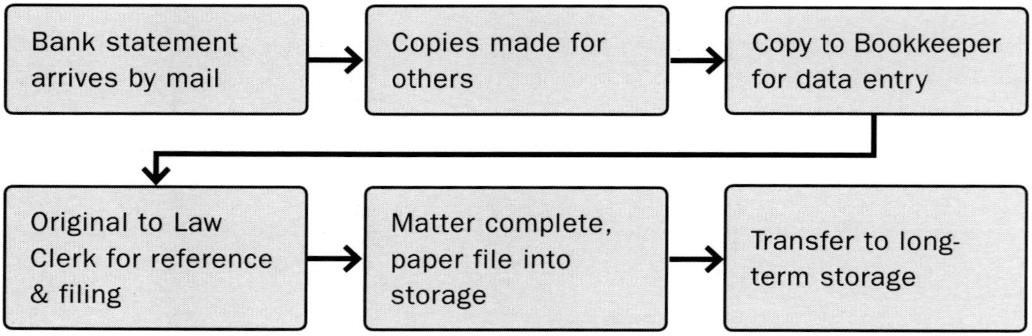

As Donna's firm transitioned to paperless, the staff changed their process to include using a Day Box, a box in the scanning area that held the original document (see Figure 1.2), which was used to check the quality of the scan and then shredded at the end of the month.

Figure 1.2 Day Box

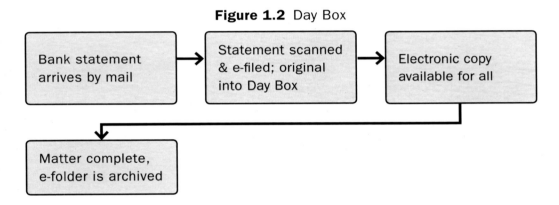

Finally, when the firm evolved to a paperless system, the monthly bank statement arrived in an electronic format, as shown in Figure 1.3.

Figure 1.3 Electronic Bank Statement

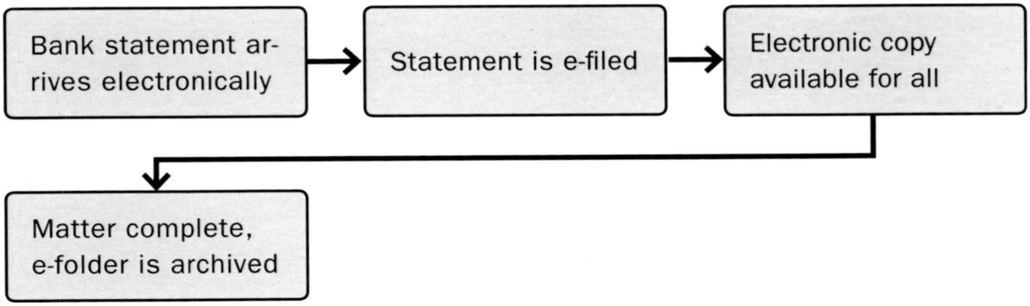

Developing the processes needed to become paperless may seem like a lot of work. But as the experience of many lawyers who have gone paperless shows, if you expend the effort to lay a solid foundation, you will be rewarded with an easier and more enjoyable transition for everyone involved.

Key Points

- Define and prioritize the specific goals you plan to achieve in going paperless. Refer to them often as you transition.
- Analyze how you handle documents in your firm. Is there a better way?

Now you know where you are and where you want to go, and you have laid the groundwork for determining what processes need to be developed to achieve your paperless goals. In Lesson 2, you will review the hardware you need.

Hardware: What You Need

You may be fortunate enough to already own all the hardware you need to forge ahead with your journey to a paperless office, or you may decide the changes you are implementing require a significant investment to upgrade or add to your existing hardware. Either way, this lesson will give you the basics of what you need to go paperless.

We do not suggest that you run out and buy every gizmo and gadget available. We realize that budgets are finite. However, we will review the four categories of hardware that are essential to running a successful paperless office:

- scanners
- servers
- backup systems
- multiple monitors or large/wide monitors

For each piece of hardware, we will tell you the most important features to look for, and we will wrap up this lesson with a helpful checklist (see Figure 2.5). Our goal is to provide the information you need to determine whether the equipment you have is up to the challenges of a paperless office, and if it is not, how to best allocate your spending money.

Scanners

You must have a high-quality scanner to convert paper documents into PDFs. PDF (Portable Document Format) is the standard format for storing electronic documents in a paperless office. (You may also have come across the acronym PDF/A, which is another PDF format intended to be suitable for the long-term preservation of documents.) We'll discuss PDFs and the software needed to create them in greater detail in Lesson 3.

Scanners are central to the paperless office. In fact, scanners will replace photocopiers in many instances. They are hard-working pieces of equipment, and you and your team will want speed and quality. And yes, we said "scanners," plural. Unless it is just you all by your lonesome, you will need more than one. Fear not: you can purchase a decent desktop scanner for less than $500. Figure 2.1 shows the must-have features.

Figure 2.1 What to Look for in a Scanner

Feature	What To Look For
Reliability	• Must stand up to heavy use • Check product information • Research reviews and particularly any complaints • Ensure adequate warranty
Sheet Feeder	• Number of sheets that can be stacked at one time • Ability to take legal size paper • Flatbed scanner slower, more labor-intensive
Speed	• Pages per minute (the more the better)
Output	• PDF/A • Fully-searchable format so can search within document for key words or phrases (otherwise can only search document name) • Default is often an image only (not searchable)

Feature	What To Look For
TWAIN-compliant	• If your scanner is TWAIN-compliant, you can scan directly to any software application that supports TWAIN. As a result, the scanned document or image appears in the application at your computer. The scanning dialog and options vary depending on the brand of scanner. • Caveat: If the scanner is not TWAIN-compliant, you will need to email the document to yourself, open it up and manually save it.
Resolution	• At least to 200 dots per inch resolution (dpi) for black and white • Gray-scale/color or OCR process requires higher resolution
Other things to consider	• Ethernet port (allowing the scanner to be directly connected to your network and accessible), AirPrint (for printing from an iOS device), duplex (double-sided) scanning, downloadable apps, size, weight

Our Two Cents on Scanners

The kind and number of scanners your office will need to go paperless depends on various factors:

- the type of law you practice
- the size of your practice
- how many of your staff will scan
- the physical layout of your office
- where scanners are best located

Scanners for the Solo Practitioner

If you are a solo practitioner, you can successfully manage with just one good desktop scanner. A very popular one is the Fujitsu ScanSnap iX500, which replaced the extremely popular and reliable ScanSnap S1500.

The Fujitsu iX500 is the sixth generation of the popular ScanSnap lineup, and it is the model you will want to buy or even upgrade to because it has several improvements over the old product. It scans 25 percent faster, and the paper moves through the scanner feed seemingly without pause. When time is of the essence, which seems to always be the case for a busy solo, the iX500 has Wi-Fi that allows you to scan to your smartphone when you're trying to leave the office. In other words, you won't have to turn your computer back on to get a copy of a document, and you can access it or e-mail it quickly. This feature alone is compelling, but another huge selling point is the fact that you can use either Macs or PCs with the iX500 (with the previous model, you had to purchase a different ScanSnap for each operating system). Type "ScanSnap iX500" into Google and you can read reviews showing how quickly this new product has gathered praise.

Scanners for Multi-Lawyer Firms

If you are not a solo, you have a few options. One is to simply have a desktop scanner for each person who will be scanning (many offices take this approach). Or you could have a mix of desktop scanners (for staff members who handle most of the documents, generally secretaries and legal assistants) and a network scanner, commonly a large multifunction copier/scanner/printer. The third option is to use only a network scanner, although that can actually decrease overall efficiency.

While you may think that you need only a network scanner or that lawyers don't need desktop scanners, this may not be the best way to proceed. When deciding what to purchase, don't discount the time-saving possibilities for each piece of equipment. A legal assistant earning $35,000 a year costs you roughly $45 an hour, including salary and overhead. When you consider the time that employees will spend going to and from the network scanner (even if it's only ten minutes a day, that's over 40 hours a year), it is more cost-efficient to install desktop scanners for about $400 each. These are real dollars saved.

Similarly, if lawyers can scan documents when they return from hearings or out-of-office appointments, it is far more efficient than giving the materials to assistants and then having to explain what the documents are.

If you're still not convinced, consider human nature. If there is only one central scanner, you will quickly hear many excuses for not scanning or waiting until many pages accumulate; and, of course, if one person is using the scanner and others are waiting, that's even more time wasted. On the other hand, if a scanner is sitting on a person's desk, there will be a greater likelihood that everything will be scanned and scanned quickly.

Scanners: So Many Choices

There are many scanners to choose from. Do a little research to narrow the selection to those that suit your needs and are within your budget. Figure 2.2 shows some we've considered and the options we like in models that were current at the time of publication, but you may find something you like even better! Check for the latest products; you will want the best equipment available when you buy it.

Figure 2.2 Scanners to Consider

Model	What We Like
HP OfficeJet Pro 8600 Plus	· all-in-one (print, scan, copy, fax) · 50-page automatic sheet feeder · connects directly to the network · all kinds of apps for it · flatbed glass scans legal size paper · touch screen display · can email directly to the printer · AirPrint compatible · a second legal-size paper tray to sit under the printer is an optional extra (but legal can usually be fed manually without the specialized legal-size tray) · Windows 7- as well as Windows XP- compatible (useful if you have older computers) · $250-$350
ScanSnap iX500 (Fujitsu)	· 50-page automatic sheet feeder · scanning speed of 25 pages per minute · small footprint · Scan wirelessly to your PC or Mac computer or iOS or Android device. · $400-$500
Fujitsu 5530C2	· 100-sheet large capacity sheet feeder · scanning speed of 50 pages per minute · handles up to 4,000 documents per day · color duplex scanning · small footprint · $2,500-$3,000

Portable Scanners

Depending upon your area of practice and how mobile you are, you may find it practical to carry a portable scanner. If you plan to scan a lot at off-site meetings, a small scanner, such as the ones made by Neat or Fujitsu, can be helpful. A USB cable connects the scanner to your computer and also supplies the power (no charging brick to carry).

Another portable scanner to check out is Doxie One. Although similar in size to the Neat scanner, the Doxie One does not require a connection to a computer when scanning. It scans anything from receipts to 8½" × 11" paper. A power adapter is included, but the machine can operate on rechargeable batteries. The Doxie One scans at eight seconds per page, syncs to an iPad, Mac, or PC, and has the ability to back up via iCloud or share through Evernote, Dropbox, or iMessage. Priced at just $149 (a wireless version is available for $199), it's worth a look at www.getdoxie.com.

When deciding which portable scanner to buy, consider the following:

- size and weight
- power source
- sheet-feeding capability
- speed
- reliability

When meeting with clients outside the office, you'll find portable scanners can be helpful for scanning materials such as a driver's license or passport, asset information, and original documents such as deeds.

Because they have built-in cameras, most smartphones and tablets can be used instead of a portable scanner. As a result, there are several scanning apps which are quite versatile and may meet your needs, while eliminating the need to buy and carry around another piece of hardware.

Servers

Invest in a dedicated server to store your firm's digital documents. Your server, coupled with a document management system—either a do-it-yourself system or a software application for organizing and managing digital documents—allows everyone connected to the server to view, annotate, and share documents and files. It also lets your staff search all files and folders quickly, so they can locate every document that contains certain terms, like "construction defect causing black mold," or has specific characteristics, such as an appellate brief before Judge Robert Smith in the Eleventh District Court of Appeals. You get the idea. Digital files stored in a searchable format on a server will exponentially increase the efficiency and effectiveness of your entire office.

There is one drawback to storing everything on a local server: when the server goes down, the whole office goes down. Of course, the same is true of any device on which you store files. To avoid this, invest wisely in a reliable server with built-in redundancy, meaning that it makes duplicate copies of data, and be sure to store at least one copy of the data off-site. See Figure 2.3 for some suggestions on what to look for in a server.

Cloud-based options such as IaaS (infrastructure as a service) and remote file servers are also viable options, as long as care is taken to provide for security, redundancy, and failover systems. You may be familiar with SaaS—software as a service—where you pay monthly for software you access over the Internet. IaaS refers to the practice of accessing a third-party's large storage system over the Internet rather than leasing, or purchasing and maintaining your own. Using IaaS eliminates the need to pay for an IT specialist to take care of an in-house server. The vendor maintains the equipment, which you pay to access monthly. IaaS facilitates remote access to files as well. For more on cloud-based storage, see Lesson 5.

Network Switch

A network switch connects all of your computers, scanners, printers, and other devices, allowing them to "talk" to each other. Because going paperless will increase the traffic over your network, you will want to have the fastest possible network switch to carry traffic speedily, which means a gigabit ethernet (GigE) switch.

Figure 2.3 What to Look for in a Server

Feature	What To Look For
Case and rack	• Accessibility • Expandability • Number of available drive bays
Form factor	• Shape and size such as tower • Consider air flow and temperature • Noise • Fan quality – you want very high quality (fan failure can result in overheating and a non-functioning computer)
Drives	• Hard drive: amount of disk space, interface • Account for expansion • Ability to continue functioning if one drive fails • Back-up • Solid state vs. rotating disk (solid state is faster and more reliable but more costly)
Memory	• How much is included • Expansion capability • Tip: Buy as much as you can afford! You won't regret it.
Network card	• Speed - GigE network card (makes file transfers and backups significantly faster) • Multiple ports for redundancy
Processor	• What is included • How many can be supported • Should be server-specific
Operating System	• Ensure it is included in the price otherwise budget for the extra cost • IT support readily available (avoid non-standard OS as it may be hard to hire knowledgeable IT support)
Power	• Redundant power supplies • Capacity of power supplies
Removable Media	• CD/DVD • Blu-ray

Use IT Support

Unless you are technologically savvy, find a qualified IT person to help you choose the right server and network switch and all that goes with them. A competent IT person can set up your server and network, maintain them, and get them up and running when you or your staff cannot. To save money, minimize support calls, and avoid being down for long periods of time while you wait for help to arrive, make sure your staff is trained by the IT person to resolve basic server or network issues. If access to local IT support is of concern, look into remote support, which can be more cost-effective but will require someone at your office to be the hands of the IT person if equipment cannot be controlled remotely.

Regular maintenance and upgrades can go a long way to minimizing downtime and expensive repairs. You should therefore budget for computer equipment to be replaced on a three- to four-year cycle. If you get more years out of the equipment than that, consider yourself lucky.

Backup Systems

This may be like confronting your worst nightmare as a lawyer, but could you cope with these scenarios?

- You turn on your computer and see the "blue screen of death."
- Your computer won't even turn on.
- Your server just went kaput.
- Your office is destroyed in a hurricane, fire, or other disaster.

If you don't have proper backup systems in place, one word comes to mind: *malpractice*. If digital materials are lost in a system failure, your computer won't be the only meltdown. Seriously, the lifeblood of your law firm is the intellectual product that resides in your client files. For years, lawyers have made copies upon copies of important paper documents to ensure the information within them is not lost. Your practice with electronic documents should be no different.

The levels of redundancies of backup systems have frequently been compared to the multiple gates and moats protecting a castle and hence a kingdom. If one fails, there are others. We recommend that you back up your computer both to an external drive or server and to secure web-based or cloud storage. This will provide three redundancies: on your computer, on your drive or server, and on the Internet. We discuss backup systems in more detail in Lesson 4.

When looking at hardware, consider the following:

- for backing up a single computer: A system that combines disk-imaging hardware with a storage device that plugs into one of your computer's USB ports and features one-button backup and restore.
- for backing up a network: Many offices use a NAS (network-attached storage) device, sometimes referred to as a "black box." This equipment allows for backing up the data on the server, which includes the software applications that reside there and all (or parts of all) users' computers.

As an example of rugged external hard drives, check the line of portable drives by ioSafe. Advertised as fireproof, waterproof, crushproof, and shockproof, ioSafe drives cost $250 and up for one terabyte capacity. The SoloPRO or SOLO G3 provides good value. Make sure that the hard drive you select will work with the fastest type of connection available on your computer. The purchase of an ioSafe hard drive includes a minimum of $2,500 data loss coverage, should it be damaged.

Multiple Monitors or Large Monitors

The benefit of multiple monitors or large (27-inch) monitors is underscored in a paperless environment: easy access to data. We suggest you need two monitors or a 27-inch monitor—at a minimum. Figure 2.4 gives some suggestions about what to look for in a monitor.

Consider how you work with paper documents spread across your desk. If you would normally have your client file open next to your computer, you'll appreciate the ability to have the digital file open on one monitor, a draft document open on a second, and possibly even a third monitor with your e-mail application open.

Consult an ergonomic specialist to help create a healthy workspace. Some people find that the improper placement of monitors can create pain in the neck and shoulders. When an ergonomic assessment was done at Sheila's office, her two monitors were replaced with one large monitor. She has had fewer problems with the new configuration. You can substitute one large monitor for two individual monitors, and view documents and other items side-by-side.

Figure 2.4 What to Look for in a Monitor

Feature	What To Look For
Definition	• Resolution is the number of pixels that can be displayed horizontally and vertically • Usable resolution limits will vary with size of monitor • Tip: High resolution on a small screen is not necessarily a good thing.
Dot pitch	• Space between the pixels • Typically .30mm to .15mm • The smaller the better
Contrast Ratios	• Don't be taken in by seemingly impressive high dynamic contrast ratios • The static contrast ratio is the one to be interested in
Refresh rate	• Number of times per second the screen is redrawn or refreshed • At least 75 Hz at the resolution you are running at • Not really a factor for LCD screens
Size	• 15" to 27" • Consider viewable size
Ergonomics options	• Tilt • Raise/lower
Connections	• Look for multiple ports such as VGA (Video Graphics Array), DVI (Digital Visual Interface), HDMI, USB ports
Onscreen Display (OSC) settings	• Adjustment of viewable settings
Warranty/Returns	• 90-day minimum money-back guarantee • Watch for restocking fees • Minimum 2-3 years parts and labor coverage • Tip: Ensure backlight and multiple pixel defects are covered by warranty.

Figure 2.5 Hardware Checklist

Scanners	
	Reliability rating for heavy office use
	Sheet feeder with ability to take legal-sized paper
	Adequate pages per minute
	PDF/A scanning as a standard setting
	Options for creating both searchable and non-searchable PDFs. Searchable PDFs have words and characters which have been OCR'd meaning that individual characters are recognized (Optical Character Recognition) and can be found during a search. A non-searchable PDF is essentially an image (like a photograph) of a page such that individual words and characters cannot be searched.
	TWAIN compliant (your scanner will be able to scan directly into any specific software application that supports the TWAIN standard. For Scrabble players: Technology Without An Important Name.)
	High resolution scanning (200 dpi for simple black and white images, or 300 dpi for OCR processing or gray-scale/color images)
	Other features: Ethernet port, duplex scanning, AirPrint, auto document feeder, cartridge cost, downloadable apps, size, weight
Servers	
	Accessible and expandable case and rack
	Shape/size and air flow and temperature
	Amount of hard drive space and ability to expand
	More than adequate memory and expansion capability
	GigE network speed
	Server-specific processor and number that can be supported
	Budget for an operating system if not included
	Capacity of power supplies
	Removable media
	Quiet operation especially if you don't have a closed server room

	External Backup Drive
	Fireproof
	Waterproof
	Ease-of-use
	Compatible connectivity with computer and operating systems
	Fast restoration of data
	TrueCrypt (free and highly secure encryption software) to secure the data on the hard drive
	Multiple Monitors
	Adequate resolution, dot pitch, static contrast ratios
	Size
	Ergonomics such as tilt and raise/lower
	Multiple ports
	Warranty/returns policy

Next, you'll want to look at the software you have and determine what you need to achieve your paperless goals in Lesson 3.

Review Software: What You Need

There really are only two software applications essential for the paperless process: (1) PDF creation software for creating electronic documents and (2) document management software for storing them in an organized fashion. Although you can locate PDF documents by searching for a word or phrase if the PDF is in a searchable format created by OCR (optical character recognition) technology, a document management system does much more than simply search. But let's begin with PDF.

PDF Creation Software

To go paperless, you'll need to convert your documents from their original formats—Microsoft Word, Excel, or PowerPoint—into digital formats that can be shared, searched, annotated, stored across computer platforms, and kept well beyond their time of creation. PDF is the standard format for these documents. Someone once quipped that PDF stands for "pretty darn fantastic," and Adobe Acrobat is the gold standard for PDF creation for the legal field.

If you are well-informed about this format, go get yourself a cookie and skip the following brief primer.

The PDF Format: A Primer

The world standard for storing and sharing documents is in the portable document format (PDF) developed by Adobe. You can read PDFs using the free Adobe Reader and many other software products, with a variety of features and costs ranging from free to expensive. Without PDF, we would be limited to sharing and storing documents in the format created by the word processing software, which is further constrained by the computer's operating system. For example, if a document was created using Word 97, it can be reviewed only on a computer with a program that can read Word 97. As software changes, earlier versions become obsolete, and newer computers may not have the ability to read older documents.

This fast-changing world of technology set the stage for a universal format that could be read on computers running different operating systems and different word processing programs. Adobe was the first to create a portable document format, or PDF. Adobe Acrobat is the program used to create the files.

For lawyers, the movement to PDFs has been led by the courts adopting e-filing systems that require documents to be filed in this format. As a result, most law firms will need and benefit from a more versatile Acrobat product, such as Acrobat Standard or Professional, to get the most benefits from going paperless.

Goal: To Share Documents across Platforms

A PDF file will easily open on most computer platforms, and there are many methods for creating PDF documents. Sharing PDFs is considerably faster than printing and faxing or mailing documents.

One of the fastest ways to create shareable PDFs uses the PDF creation feature built into most current versions of word processing software:

- In Corel WordPerfect, select *Publish to PDF* from the **File** menu.
- In Microsoft Word, select *Save as PDF* from the **File** menu.
- In Apple Pages, using the **Share and Print** tool, select *Send as PDF*.
- In Office2 HD, choose *PDF Format* from the **Export Format** field.

Goal: To Send Documents in a Secured Unalterable Version

Lawyers frequently send important documents in a secured "locked-down" version so recipients can't open them up and convert them back to an easily altered word-processed version. Can you imagine the mayhem that would ensue if you sent a settlement agreement in an unlocked PDF to an unethical opposing counsel who opened it, altered it, and then signed and returned it?

There are many programs available that claim to convert PDF documents into Word or WordPerfect. You may find this troublesome if you are a litigator. And if you are a transactional lawyer e-mailing PDFs of estate planning documents or contracts you don't want altered, the thought of them being changed without your involvement may be a concern. Fortunately, many PDF tools allow you to lock down a file so it cannot be altered. To have this level of security, you will need to use Adobe Acrobat or a competing product. Look for this important feature when shopping for PDF creation software.

Goal: To File Your Court Documents Electronically via E-filing

While the majority of courts accept electronic files as PDFs, others are moving to a more secure standard, PDF/A, which prevents changes to the documents; unfortunately, the use of PDF/A also prevents you from applying OCR to the documents, which can be a big hassle.

PDF/A was developed for preserving and archiving documents, thereby ensuring that users will be able to access them for many years to come. The version lawyers need to use is PDF/A-1b, which meets the requirements of most courts. Many software programs have a simple means for selecting PDF/A-1b compliance, which makes the conversion process easy. To convert a PDF to the PDF/A standard, open the PDF file in Adobe Acrobat X or XI; then, under the **File** menu, select **Save As**, which opens a new drop-down. Choose **More Options** and then **PDF/A**. You can also convert your documents to PDF/A with recent versions of either Microsoft Word or Corel WordPerfect, but use caution: you may find the default is regular PDF. If you want to regularly save to PDF/A, change the default to PDF/A, if possible.

Documents saved as PDF/A files under the International Organization for Standardization's (ISO) standard for electronic documents should be as readable in fifteen or twenty-five years as they are today. Saving documents as PDF/A files "flattens out" attachments. However, any embedded audio or video clips will be removed; thus, while PDF/A allows a file to be stored longer, it does remove some items that you may also want to retain. We recommend that when saving a document in this format you include the designation PDF/A in the filename so you can preserve the original with any graphic images, audio, videos, hyperlinks, footnotes, form fields, or other interactive elements that are flattened or stripped out of your document when saved as a PDF/A.

Although Adobe invented PDFs and has the market-leading PDF creation program, Adobe Acrobat, there are other applications that can create PDF documents. Look at the list of features to evaluate the cost for what you need. See Figure 3.1 for a chart listing some of the other programs you may want to consider.

Figure 3.1 Programs for Creating PDF Files

Software	Features	Platform/Cost
Adobe Acrobat XI Pro	• Bates stamping • Combine files into PDF Portfolio • Control & protect with passwords • Create Interactive files with audio, video (Adobe Flash Player compatible) • Create PDF files- convert from MS Word, Excel, & PowerPoint; Print to PDF select Adobe PDF as your Printer; Scan to PDF; Convert HTML pages to PDF for archiving website • Create electronic forms • Edit PDF Files- text & images • Electronically sign & certify • Export from PDF files – convert to MS Word, Excel, & PowerPoint • Redaction • SharePoint integration • Versioning comparisons	• PDF/A-1b compliant • Windows & Mac OS. • $449.00/1 user. • Volume licensing program available.
Nitro Pro 8	• Bates stamping • Control & protect with passwords • Convert & export • Create electronic forms • Create PDFs from MS Word, Excel, & PowerPoint • Edit text & images • Electronically sign & certify • Redaction • Scan & Optical Character Recognition (OCR)	• PDF/A-1b compliant • Windows-based only. • $119.99/1 user. • Volume licensing program available.
PDF Converter Pro 8 (Nuance)	• Bates stamping • Control & protect with passwords • Convert & export • Create electronic forms • Create PDFs from Corel WordPerfect, MS Word, Excel, & PowerPoint • Edit text & images • Electronically sign & certify • Redaction	• PDF/A-1b compliant • Windows & Mac OS. • $99.99/1 user. • Volume licensing program available. • Enterprise version available.

You may choose Adobe Acrobat simply because there are so many users that you can easily find someone to answer a question. Adobe also does a good job of supporting users by providing free instructions, including the popular blog *Acrobat for Legal Professionals (http://blogs.adobe.com/ acrolaw/)*, in which Rick Borstein shares tips and videos on how to accomplish some of the more complicated projects.

Document Management System Software

Without question, your paperless office will benefit dramatically by using a document management system (DMS) to store, track, and access the flood of information received and generated.

You probably already have a system in place for managing your paper documents. You also likely have a structure for organizing whatever electronic documents you have. A good DMS takes you a step further and directs you in how to organize your electronic files and how to name the documents you create or scan.

If you are purchasing a system, it will typically have built-in protocols for naming documents, which include the type of document, when it was created, and who created it. With many systems, there is little ability for serious deviation. Worldox and HP WorkSite are two of the best-known DMS applications hosted on your office server, and they permit you to customize their interfaces to your specific needs.

You can also build your own document management system to organize your electronic files and consistently name these stored documents. The most difficult task in doing so is strictly adhering to the naming convention. With a homegrown DMS, you will not have the ability to thwart serious deviation that has the potential to destroy your well-thought-out process. If you expect there will be strong, possibly insurmountable, resistance to using a standardized naming system for files and folders, seriously consider investing in commercial software. Such software imposes a DMS structure that cannot be altered. In addition, if documents will be accessed by more than two or three people, purchasing a DMS may be a better option, since file naming may become cumbersome when there are many authors. This is why firms with more than twenty or thirty users often opt for purchasing a DMS that has built-in enforcement of naming protocols.

Document management systems can be indispensable to firms that need to share a knowledge base of documents. For example, lawyers share forms and templates of documents, and DMS makes this far easier to do. Thus, if a lawyer needs to draft a complicated trust provision in an estate plan, he or she can simply access and search the DMS database to find examples of similar documents previously created.

Worldox

Worldox is the most well-known DMS, and it has been the leader in the small-to-medium law office market, with little competition. Once installed and set up, Worldox manages all types of documents and files, including e-mail, voice-mail records, and video files. It is easy for lawyers and staff to use and is affordable for small and midsize firms. With the growing use of iPads by lawyers, Worldox has developed a free iPad app for users of Worldox GX2 or GX3 and Worldox/Web Mobile.

iManage

Autonomy iManage WorkSite, formerly Interwoven, requires dedicated personnel and front-end customization for successful implementation and upgrades, which is why the product is more commonly used by larger firms. This DMS offers highly sophisticated search and categorization of electronically stored information found across the typical enterprise, including e-mails, instant messages, videos, and audio files.

SaaS Cloud-Based DMS

Affordable document management systems are provided as SaaS from the Internet. Here are some of the available options:

- Box for Business provides password-protected links to documents and allows you to limit how long someone has access to a file by link deactivation or file deletion.

- Cabinet offers SAFE as traditional installed DMS software and SAFE CLOUD accessed as a subscription from the Internet.

- NetDocuments has two redundant world-class data centers for storing information securely and offers an additional service to maintain a backup at the customer's site using ND Local Document Services, a reassuring option that may be worth the extra cost.

- nQueue Billback's iA Virtual Cabinet offers easy integration with Microsoft Outlook, Word, and Excel and greater version control by allowing documents to be easily retracted when sent through the portal.

- Worldox GX3 is available as a desktop version, an enterprise version for your on-site data center, or a SaaS-hosted cloud version accessed from the Internet.

Practice management and accounting systems like Time Matters, Amicus Attorney, and PCLaw all have DMS components. It is not a main feature of most of these systems; however, some practice management products may meet your document management needs, so you should evaluate those features before jumping in to buy a DMS. While many practice management products are not robust enough to meet the needs of a paperless law office, some will work quite well. One of our colleagues, for example, uses Legal Files, whose document management features are fairly robust, so it pays to shop around.

When looking for a DMS, don't be tempted by all the bells and whistles. Make sure the application has the features you need, and don't pay for those you will likely never use. Before making a purchase commitment, do your homework, read the reviews, and speak to others who work in offices similar to yours about their experiences with the software. Take advantage of any free trials so you can give the software a test run before investing.

Cost of DMS Options

The cost of an off-the-shelf DMS includes the purchase price or subscription cost as well as training and ongoing support and maintenance—and training is essential. The current price for Worldox GX3 Professional is $425 for each concurrent user with an annual maintenance fee of $88 per concurrent user. Support for nonmaintenance users is $300 per incident. By comparison, SaaS or cloud-based DMS software allows you to pay as you go, which makes it affordable for most users. As an example, the current price for NetDocuments Professional Plus Edition is $38 per user per month.

Do-It-Yourself DMS

For those considering developing their own version of a DMS, Donna estimates that the staff time alone to develop her firm's DIY DMS was between $12,000 and $15,000. This cost was spread over several years, and, other than the time to periodically tweak the system, the development cost is over. Donna's firm is also not paying for ongoing monthly or yearly subscription fees. At the time her law office went paperless, it was composed of one lawyer and four staff members. Keep in mind that if you have staff and create your own system, you may encounter a potential hidden cost from noncompliance by one or more staff members. Donna had this problem, which increased the overall cost of her firm's DMS.

While it likely would have been less expensive to purchase commercial software at the beginning, Donna wouldn't have a system that is tailored perfectly to her firm and is the backbone of her paperless office.

In the Appendix, you will find a DMS file-naming system from Donna and one from a colleague of ours, Daniel Siegel. By looking at these and considering others, you may adopt or adapt one or you may get an idea for still another approach that works better for your firm. In addition, see Figure 3.2 below for a quick comparison of DIY DMS and off-the-shelf DMS. SaaS options are essentially the same as off-the-shelf options except they are accessed on a subscription basis from the Internet.

Figure 3.2 DMS: DIY versus Off-the-Shelf and SaaS

	DIY DMS	Off-the-shelf DMS & SaaS
Compliance	Only if staff are willing to jump on the paperless bandwagon.	Is absolute so staff can't derail the paperless project by refusal to comply.
Compatibility	Runs on whatever system you use for development (Mac, Windows, Linux).	May run on on only one platform. (Windows or Mac); check compatibility before deciding. Compatibility issues not likely for SaaS systems which are accessed from Internet.
Portability	If the firm splits, easy for each lawyer to continue the system in separate offices. Just need to decide who gets what file or gets duplicates of what documents.	May be problematic and may need to hire an expert to accomplish.
Expandability	If the firm grows, no increased cost other than training. If firm grows beyond 10-12 people, compliance will be more problematic.	Easy to expand, just buy more licences. Due to per seat subscription fees, costs grows as firm grows.
Adaptability	Can customize to the way you work but can be "too adaptable" (see compliance).	You will need to adjust to the structure although there may be some options.

You'll want to look in Lesson 4 for a discussion of the protocols needed in a paperless office.

Establish Paperless Protocols and Improve Your Business Practices

We all have procedures for how we accomplish tasks in our offices. Protocols describe the precise manner in which these tasks must be consistently performed by everyone. Having protocols for handling your law office's important paper and electronic documents should help you improve your business practices.

You will likely not want to waste time and money converting documents in closed files or even current files to PDF. Instead, choose a specific date and put your time and effort into converting all new files from that date forward.

If you want to scan closed files to reduce storage costs, investigate whether a local copying/scanning company will do this on a more affordable basis if they can have a long period of time to complete the work. Some scanning companies will give you a better price if they can have the flexibility to complete your project during downtime between their bigger jobs.

Converting Documents to PDF

You will need to develop a protocol for converting paper documents and electronic documents from other formats to PDF. Develop a written process that, at a minimum, outlines when a document will be converted to PDF, who will do it, and what will be done with the original.

You should always convert documents to PDF when they arrive at your office so you won't be overwhelmed by the volume to be converted and abandon your plan to become paperless. Although the whole office team should be comfortable converting documents to PDF, appoint one or two people to have the primary responsibility—usually these are the staff who handle all incoming documents. Other team members will need to know how to scan, name, and store various documents they work with, including e-mails, in PDF.

Create and use a colored stamp to indicate that a document has been scanned so anyone looking at an original can quickly determine whether it has been scanned.

Ensuring Quality Control

It is important to have a quality control system to ensure scanning is done accurately. While most scanners are remarkably reliable and accurate, none are perfect, and there are no do-overs once a paper document has been shredded. A frequent problem is missing or skewed pages from operator or machine error. A quality control system can catch these errors and the document can be re-scanned to rectify them.

In Donna's firm, their centralized scanner attaches the scanned document to an e-mail that is sent to the staff person who will be working with the document. To reduce errors, the person doing the scanning must include the total page count of the document being scanned in the subject line of the e-mail so the recipient can verify that all pages were included.

Other firms have a team member assigned to verify scanned documents by comparing them with the originals. This is a fast process of sitting in front of a monitor and quickly ascertaining that all pages have been captured and are readable and that the scanned document is named properly. Anyone who has been involved in quality checking document coding will be helpful in working out a quality control checklist and protocol for scanning.

Storing Before Shredding

Store paper copies for a specific length of time to verify the accuracy and quality of their scanned digital format. As previously mentioned, Donna uses a Day Box to temporarily store paper documents and has an official policy that the contents will be shredded six months after the day the box was used. This provides considerable peace of mind for everyone, especially for those who were hesitant to give up paper.

Your protocol should have a consistent period of time to hold on to original documents after they have been scanned. It would be prudent to retain the originals for at least thirty days. A system similar to the one Donna uses would be very helpful as a safeguard against accidentally destroying a document before it has been properly preserved.

Creating a File-Naming System

Every electronic document, once scanned or converted to PDF, must be named in a standardized, consistent manner. You'll want to devise a file-naming system that makes sense for the number of staff in your firm, and the documents worked on. The filename should contain just enough details so any team member knows what a document is without having to open it. In the Appendix, we share two sample document-naming systems, but there are many ways to approach this.

Document management systems you buy as installed software or subscribe to as a cloud-based SaaS usually have a standardized file-naming convention built into them, which serves as a great starting point for your office's own system. However, depending upon what DMS you adopt, file-naming protocols may be helpful.

Organizing Document Storage

For your firm to benefit from going paperless, you need to network all of its computers; in other words, all files should be stored on a central server that everyone can access. Most law firms set up their electronic filing cabinets to mimic their traditional filing cabinets. Your protocol should specify how your files, folders, and subfolders will be named and organized.

It is best to always open a new matter file for returning clients. If you organize by client and matters, it will be easier to manage your document retention and destruction procedures (if you don't create a super client file spanning several years and several different matters). If you set matters up as subfolders under a single client folder, you will want to designate the destruction date on each matter subfolder and indicate this on your file inventory.

When deciding how many subfolders you need, aim for only a screen's worth of files in any subfolder. If the list will exceed a screen, consider whether an additional subfolder is needed. The extra scrolling time you avoid may not seem like a lot, but when multiplied by the number of times a day you encounter it and by the number of staff in your firm, the lost time adds up quickly.

When naming subfolders, pay attention to how they will be sorted. For example, beginning all correspondence folders with "Corr" will allow them to be grouped together when displayed in the index. (See the Appendix for further details.)

Use Templates to Ensure Consistency

Once the folder structure is determined, create a "folder template," or a set of standard folders and subfolders, for each type of matter handled by your firm; this saves time and ensures consistent naming. Keep your folder templates where they can be easily found and copied.

To protect a template file from being accidentally changed, make it read-only. To make a Word document read-only, open the file and follow these steps:

1. Click *File*, then *Save* (or *Save As* if previously saved).
2. Click *Tools* (near the bottom of the screen to the left of *Save*).
3. Click *General Options*.
4. Click to put a check in the box beside *Read-only recommended*.
5. Click *OK*.
6. Save the file.

Backing Up and Test Restoring

A paperless office should have multilayered, reliable, and frequent backups, including incremental and full backups, and on-site and off-site backups. Technology is a wonderful tool, but nothing is fail-safe. The integrity of your backup system should be checked by regularly performing a test restore to ensure your data is preserved in a usable form and restorable with minimum delay and difficulty.

The best way to determine how often you should back up your data is by asking yourself what you can afford to lose. At a minimum, you will want to back up more than once a day; many systems (both on- and off-site) will provide for more frequent or continuous backups. Your system should allow for this.

The safest course is to have multiple backup redundancies. Back up your data on your computer hard drive because software applications can freeze up, resulting in lost data. Back up your data on your firm's server because it is a more powerful storage center. Back up on something away from your physical office, especially secure Internet or cloud-based storage, in case of a natural disaster.

Part of your law firm's disaster plan should be to have your data backed up and accessible to you when you reach safety. The devastation of powerful storms such as Katrina and, more recently, Sandy caused many law firms to use safe, secure storage on the Internet; if a firm's infrastructure is lost or inaccessible, the data can still be accessed through a secure Internet connection from anywhere. The post-disaster stories of lawyers accessing their law firm's data from the Internet once they relocated to safe areas illustrate that the cloud can be a valuable component of a backup plan. Lawyers who had this accessibility resumed their practices sooner. We will discuss cloud-based storage in more detail in Lesson 5.

If your firm has only your stand-alone computer, you'll want to back up to an external storage device that plugs into one of your computer's USB ports and use a secure cloud-based storage system as well.

Why all these layers? If something happens to the first layer, you can still get back your data from the second, and so on. Although they are rare, we have all heard the horror stories of people needing their backup only to find it has gone awry in some fashion. Don't tempt the odds. We'd much rather have a backup we never need than need one and not have it available.

Managing the Size of Data Storage

As you accumulate more and more electronic files, backups can become unnecessarily huge, which slows down the process and requires additional space, costing time and money. Here are some suggestions to reduce file size and maximize the capacity of data storage:

- Set the scanner to a lower resolution, such as 200 or 300 dpi.
- Set the Adobe Acrobat function to reduce file size.
- Set the scanner to black-and-white scanning.

Closing and Storing Files

For paper client files, a good file closure process goes through the complete file, looking for and removing

- original documents belonging to the client,
- sample documents from other matters, and
- duplicate copies.

You should review a digital file prior to storage with the same level of care you would use for a paper file. Focus on storing the file in a manner that will best preserve it for the length of time it must be saved. Essentially, you are archiving your file. As discussed elsewhere, the safest format in which to store digital files is PDF (or PDF/A), which is the international standard. If you don't think this is important, consider that opening a document stored in its native format, such as Microsoft Word 98, would require having a computer capable of reading or running Microsoft Word 98. Using PDF will save you headaches should you need access to a digital file or document.

Creating a File Retention Schedule

Your jurisdiction or governing body will have guidelines for how long client files should be retained. Some files may need to be kept for set periods of time based on your jurisdiction's equivalent to ABA Model Rule 1.15 (Safekeeping Property). This rule requires preservation of client property for five years from the date the matter is closed.

Most jurisdictions define client property as including not only all client trust account records but also the actual client file. Others conclude that if you provide your client with a full copy of the client file, then what you hold in the office is the law firm's property.

Do your due diligence and check your jurisdiction's rules. Does your jurisdiction require that the law firm maintain a complete paper file for the duration of the client matter? If so, then your protocol will need to be paperless upon completion. How long should you preserve a digital version of the client file? Arguably, for the same length of time you would preserve the paper version. How long this needs to be will depend upon various factors, such as ethical, legal, and professional considerations and economic and practical issues.

Find out if your jurisdiction has a statute of ultimate repose on a legal malpractice claim. This is the outer limitation on when a malpractice claim can be brought. It makes sense to hold on to your client file for the duration of this period in case you need it to defend yourself. If you don't have insurance, be even more careful to preserve the client file. Check for any guidelines or policies from your state bar or law society and your malpractice insurer, if you have one.

Finally, it is now considered best practice to disclose to clients that your office is paperless and to explain what your firm's storage protocols are. In addition, you should disclose that if a client requests a copy of the client file, or a portion of it, you will provide the information electronically. If you don't do so, the rules in your jurisdiction may require you to print the file.

Destroying Electronic Records

Storage space for digital files is affordable; however, adopt a unified business practice of safeguarding both paper and digital files for the required time period and then safely destroying them. Remember that when you delete an electronic document, it is still there. To destroy digital data on a local storage device, use a software program such as Darik's Boot and Nuke, which completely obliterates the data. Before storing digital data on a third-party site, find out how destruction can be completed. At some point, your law practice will come to an end due to retirement, incapacity, death, or some other reason. While you may be required to preserve your client data (in whatever form), you still need to set a specified time for it to be destroyed or wiped from any remote server.

Developing Knowledge Management

Give some thought as to how you will organize your resource and research materials, which may contain a vast amount of documents, including e-books and e-publications. You might want to copy and scan the tables of contents from your physical books and include them in your knowledge management system as well.

Training Your Staff

This seems like it would be obvious, but anecdotal evidence suggests otherwise. Ongoing training of staff members ensures your future team is as much onboard as your original team. You should also spot-check client files to determine whether your staff is following procedures and complying with protocols.

Well-trained staff should never have to guess how to name a document or where to save it. If this happens, it usually means a protocol needs updating or isn't clear enough. Guessing could result in the document becoming lost amidst all of the other files.

Reviewing and Revising for Efficiency

Review and revise your paperless protocols as your firm changes or as processes appear to be working less efficiently than planned. Initially, you will likely want to conduct reviews of your protocols at thirty, sixty, and ninety days. Once you are satisfied with your system, an annual review will keep it running at peak performance.

When developing protocols, take advantage of all available resources. Your state bar association or law society will likely be able to assist you in developing policies for the closure, retention, and destruction of client files, including paper and digital documents, and may have a practice management adviser to answer your specific questions.

Do not allow shortcuts on established protocols. They are set up for the firm's safety.

Now that you know what it takes to establish the paperless protocols you need, and are planning your backup redundancies, you'll want to look closely at using storage services on the Internet.

Take a Closer Look at Cloud-Based Storage

Cloud-based storage can be valuable as one of the layers of backup redundancies for your data. With advances in mobile technology, cloud-based systems are now an essential component of online document collaboration—with out-of-office lawyers and staff, as well as clients. They are a boon for online project management. Lawyers find the ability to sync and store files across platforms from the other side of town (or another continent) supports having a mobile practice. Improved workflow is enhanced by the efficiencies that are a by-product of choosing cloud-based storage to reduce paper or go paperless. But approach these services wisely. If you plan to use cloud-based storage, there are several caveats.

Your first step should be to check whether your jurisdiction has issued an ethics opinion regarding cloud storage of client materials. In the Resources section of this book, you will find a link to cloud ethics opinions around the United States. Read these rules and opinions carefully and select a service provider that can comply with your jurisdiction's ethical requirements. In your written fee agreement or engagement letter, be sure to fully inform clients that you use cloud storage. Clients should give informed consent to online storage of confidential file materials.

When reviewing cloud storage or web-based storage options, keep in mind that you have an ethical and fiduciary duty to protect your clients' property. You are responsible for any third parties' actions or policies that violate rules. Prudent best practices include the use of encryption software, such as TrueCrypt, Folder Lock, or SafeGuard, before trusting your data to the cloud. Most cloud providers encrypt your data during transmission. If your data is already encrypted when you upload it, you are making sure it is far safer. Are there any guarantees? No—but encryption will increase the security of your data and ensure compliance with ethical rules about protecting client confidentiality and client property.

Finally, do your due diligence and look closely at the cloud provider's website to get a good idea of who you may be dealing with. This might bring to mind a *New Yorker* cartoon of a dog surfing the web with the caption: "On the Internet no one knows you're a dog." You would not store client files in a dilapidated shed that is missing its door or doesn't have a functioning lock, so look beyond the home page to determine if this service provider will meet your needs and protect your clients' materials. Some providers offer additional assurance to users by having a third party review their security practices and by complying with strict outside standards.

You may see more and more reviews by eTrust, SysTrust, TRUSTe, Trustwave, and VeriSign and certifications that a service provider is HIPAA/HITECH compliant. But don't be fooled by a logo touting SAS 70 certification; there is none. In the United States, SSAE 16 complies with auditing standards from the American Institute of CPAs (AICPA), which provides greater parity with the international audit standard of ISAE 3402. Still higher is a designation known as the SOC (Service Organization Control) 2 (or SOC 3) report, which means stronger sets of controls and requirements of data center service organizations and allows benchmark comparisons. You should see this information displayed prominently and explained on the service provider's website.

Here are some areas of inquiry and questions to ask when choosing a cloud service provider.

Security

1. What security does the service provider have in place for protecting data in its custody?

2. Is the security touted as bank-grade or military level or higher? This likely means the vendor has adopted multiple security layers with 256-bit data encryption used by financial institutions—the highest Internet security available. It is not a standard but sounds more impressive than saying "as good as it gets." Your best bet is to look for SOC 2 or SOC 3 reporting, which indicates reliable benchmarked standards intended to evaluate data center audits.

3. Is data encrypted while stored?

4. Is data encrypted during transmission to or from the site with at least 128-bit SSL encryption?

5. Does anyone hold the encryption key besides you?

6. Can anyone in the service provider's company access your material?

7. Will the service provider hand over your data to anyone besides you without your verified consent?

8. If a security breach occurs, will you be notified in a timely fashion?

9. Are physical servers in multiple secure centers in your own country?

10. Are physical servers in data centers certified by SOC 2 or SOC 3 reporting?
11. What data security and recovery testing does the service provider conduct regularly?
12. Does the provider have a third party certify its services?

Keep in mind that there is a need for greater international standards to ensure that data storage centers are secure and data integrity is maintained; current certifications and representations may not be sufficient.

Privacy

1. What information is kept about you and for what purpose?
2. Will the service provider release any information about you to third parties?
3. If the provider ever receives a subpoena demanding information, will it notify you before complying?

Other

1. If a bankruptcy occurs or the site is closed, is it clear that your data is not an asset of the service provider and is not subject to seizure by or for the site's creditors?
2. What notification will you receive if the site must cease operations?
3. Will the service provider assist you in retrieving your data from its server?
4. What assurance will the service provider give that, if you request it, your data has been securely wiped from all its servers, including any backup tapes, drives, or other devices?

5. If you need to terminate service, how long will it take for your data to be securely removed from the provider's server?

6. If your service is canceled due to your failure to make timely payments, how long will you have access to your data so you can retrieve it?

7. Will you keep a local copy of your cloud data?

Terms of Service

Carefully read the terms of service of any cloud provider's agreement. It will likely contain many provisions beyond these lists. If you don't understand a provision, ask for clarification. Select cloud-based storage with proper care and give more consideration to providers focused on serving the needs of businesses, especially those businesses subject to stringent security and privacy considerations.

Next, you'll want to look closely at ways to get buy-in from all the stakeholders in your firm regarding a paperless office. Some tips for getting commitment from your team are in Lesson 6.

How to Get Commitment from Your Team and Buy-in from All Stakeholders

You now know the nuts and bolts needed to create a paperless office. Besides having the right tools, another key step is getting everyone's commitment. Resistance from even one person can seriously hamper the chances of success.

It is easy to understand an attachment to paper: it is tangible and familiar. There are systems in place to deal with it. The idea of changing all of this often provokes anxiety.

You may need to do some hard selling to persuade your paper-loving staff and colleagues to adopt a paperless office. Involving people at every step of the way will lead to faster buy-in. Your positive attitude will be contagious and help with persuasion.

In this lesson, we'd like to share what we have learned about the importance of commitment and offer practical tips to help you achieve full support. Begin your paperless journey by focusing on these four things:

- becoming a positive role model
- involving your staff at every step
- ensuring you have complete compliance
- preparing yourself to deal with naysayers

Becoming a Positive Role Model

Others will look to you for guidance and support in the process of going paperless, so you need to show that you are positive and excited about the upcoming changes. Your enthusiasm will be infectious, and your attitude will play a key role in inspiring everyone to willingly make the change.

When Donna took her office paperless in 2006, she endeavored to keep motivation and excitement high by getting people to stay focused on the ultimate goals they were working toward and the positive benefits that going paperless would bring. She is convinced this contributed a great deal to the ultimate success.

Part of being a good leader involves understanding the people you are leading. Look for those who are enthusiastic promoters of new ideas. They will help you win the support of anyone who may be hesitant but not averse to change. What is in it for them? They will need to be shown the benefits that going paperless will bring to them personally.

In their paper "Managing the Transition to Paperless" (presented at ABA TECHSHOW 2012), Russell Alexander and David Bilinsky suggest that as change occurs, three distinct groupings will emerge within your firm: Enthusiasts, Backbones, and Resisters. Watch as these groups become apparent in your office. Here are some tips to help you deal effectively with each:

1. **Enthusiasts.** This group recognizes the benefits of change; they are eager to help spread and support the new way of doing things. Feed their enthusiasm and use it to your advantage to help sway those who are resistant.

2. **Backbones.** Members of this group make up the majority. They are solid, consistent performers and are supportive of the changes you are implementing. Rely on their consistency. Try to convert a few into Enthusiasts. Obviously the more Enthusiasts and Backbones you have, the easier the transition will be.

3. **Resisters.** This group is opposed to the changes, due to perceived loss of power and/or status. They also do not care to expend the energy to effect change. Resisters can have significant power over others. Do your best to convince them of the benefits of going paperless.

Involving Your Staff at Every Step

By transitioning to paperless, you are asking your staff and colleagues to embrace radical changes, which can be a difficult and anxiety-ridden process for some. Your job is to make this transition smooth and painless. Involvement is the key. In our experience, if team members are involved early on and stay involved throughout, the transition will go much more smoothly, and compliance will be greater. Paperless processes should be created by those who use them, rather than imposed by those who do not.

To get everyone involved when introducing paperless practices in your firm, regular team meetings are a must. Here's how to make the most of those meetings.

1. Encourage open and honest sharing of ideas and concerns.

2. Report on the status of implementing the new processes.

3. Brainstorm ideas for improvements or solving problems.

4. Schedule weekly meetings initially, reduce frequency gradually, and eliminate when no longer needed.

5. Insist on full attendance as scheduled to keep momentum and unity.

If enthusiasm wanes, think of creative ways to turn things around and keep everyone involved. For example, hold a contest for the best paperless tip of the week, give movie tickets for the most paper saved in a week, or have a pizza lunch for a specific goal reached.

Ensuring You Have Complete Compliance

A paperless office cannot succeed unless there is full participation by every person. Without compliance across the board, you will be fighting a losing battle. Be mindful that negative reactions to going paperless may develop into noncompliance, whether blatant or clandestine, with your new processes.

Check regularly to ensure that all new procedures are being followed and that all staff are using the new system. Some people can be so averse to change that they will do almost anything to avoid it. This can lead to the sabotage of your early efforts.

If you encounter resistance, try to find out what's causing it.

- Is it based on a misperception that jobs will be cut if the paperless project proves successful? If so, assure your staff that if both the quality and quantity of work increase and the bottom line improves, there need not be personnel reductions. Stress that benefits such as the opportunity to work from home may become possible.

- Is it a fear of the unknown? When a staff member approaches you with concerns, listen carefully and consider if improvements or changes may be appropriate. Repeatedly remind your staff and colleagues of the goals you are all working toward and the positive benefits to be achieved.

Regularly schedule meetings to discuss how things are going, air concerns, and address any problems that may arise.

Spot-check to determine whether new processes are being implemented properly. Incentives such as prizes or luncheons are just two of the rewards you can give if processes are being followed and milestones reached.

We have all heard of studies and had experiences validating this very important point: rollout of technology is critical to adoption. However, human nature balks at change that disrupts the level of comfort gained in familiarity. In many law offices, there are software programs that have languished because training was insufficient or nonexistent. We can't emphasize enough the need to provide adequate training for new software and hardware. Investing in training is always money well spent. It will help achieve full compliance and get your team up to speed quickly, reducing frustration, increasing productivity, and improving the bottom line.

Preparing Yourself to Deal with Any Naysayers

As you journey to paperless, you will likely encounter a naysayer or two. Address their concerns when possible so they do not sow the seeds of dissention and doubt.

Although you shouldn't have to justify your decision to go paperless, you can save yourself some grief by deciding in advance how you will respond if challenged. The reasons you will hear about why you should not go paperless will run the gamut, from the lack of a paper trail to the shortcomings of technology to security threats and everything in between. Some concerns are valid and need to be addressed. Others can be reasonably refuted or rebutted. None of them should cause you to abandon your pursuit of the paperless office.

If you don't convert the naysayers, they may become saboteurs. These persons would be a better fit at a traditional paper-based law firm, and your program will be more likely to succeed without them.

You'll want to look closely at your system in Lesson 7 as you do some fine-tuning.

Lesson 7

Fine-Tune Your System: Focus on the Details

Some of the processes described below, such as sharing electronic files safely, are integral to the proper functioning of your paperless office; others, such as digital signatures and e-faxing, will enable you to personalize and get the most out of your paperless office. As you discover methods to do things more efficiently, you will want to continually fine-tune your processes.

Sharing Electronic Files

As you go paperless and work increasingly with electronic documents, you will need to find new ways to safely share information with others, inside and outside your firm.

Start by looking at how and what you share. Consider these questions:

1. How are documents shared within your physical office?
2. What happens when a lawyer or staff person is working outside the office, such as at a courthouse, on a business trip, or at an off-site meeting?

3. How do you provide documents to clients, other lawyers, or anyone else outside your firm?

4. When you collaborate on a presentation with a colleague across the state or across the country, how is sharing accomplished?

5. If you litigate, what are the requirements of your court system for the e-filing of materials?

6. Identify all of the ways information arrives at or leaves your office, including paper mail, faxing, e-mail, and by courier. How much of this could be accomplished electronically?

7. How do your existing methods fit with your new paperless procedures?

8. Where must process adjustments be made?

9. Does your jurisdiction have rules about data being stored in other countries? If so, do you know where cloud-based services are storing your data?

Security should be your number one concern. Your clients' data must remain secure and confidential. Ensure that any data in transit or stored is properly encrypted and can be accessed only by the intended recipients. Review your governing body's rules to ensure that you comply with any regulations and follow any guidelines about information sharing.

Using Data-Sharing Services

There are many services available to help you share data and documents with others. Some are cloud storage services, and others are a means to securely send files that are too big to attach to an e-mail. Here are some of the more popular services:

- Adobe Sendnow
- Box
- Dropbox
- Filesanywhere
- FolderShare
- Google Drive
- MediaFire
- SkyDrive
- SugarSync
- Hightail (formerly YouSendIt)

Before signing up with one of these services, research not just the cost but the specific features and security you need. Consider, also, whether you want automatic syncing of revisions, a function offered by some, but not all, of these companies. Size limitations may be an issue if you regularly send large files. Whatever service you choose, the goal is to keep your firm's data confidential and encrypted.

Creating a File-Sharing Policy

Develop a file-sharing policy for your firm. Some of the issues you will want to address include the following:

1. How and when may electronic information be sent from the firm and by whom?
2. Exactly what can be shared and in what format? In PDF only or in Word, Excel, and other original formats?
3. What level of permissions should be set for various documents?
4. What about metadata? When should it be stripped before sharing?

5. What do you anticipate recipients will do with files? Mark up the documents and return them for editing? Edit the original documents with or without track changes or comments?

Once developed, the policy should be reviewed with your entire staff to ensure they understand the importance of sending out electronic data safely and securely.

Connecting and Collaborating

More lawyers are using various desktop-sharing tools to connect and collaborate with staff, clients, or colleagues in other locations. Several software options are available. Both LogMeIn and GoToMyPC offer desktop sharing as a feature. Mikogo allows you to share your computer screen with up to twenty-five participants simultaneously. Mikogo requires a business license if you use it for business or commercial purposes. There are several purchase options, depending upon the number of participants and a one-time fee option. CrossLoop screen-sharing software offers some features that are similar to Mikogo, but the free version is limited to two participants. There is also a fee-based version of CrossLoop (Pro) with additional features.

Addressing Security

Security is essential, but it is even more critical when using Wi-Fi hot spots in hotels, airports, coffeehouses, and various other public areas. At a minimum, every device you use should be protected with a strong password of sixteen characters, using a variety of uppercase and lowercase letters, numbers, symbols, and special characters. More and more lawyers rely on password keepers that also have the ability to generate strong passwords. Many of these tools have an app so they can sync with computers, tablets, and smartphones. Some popular password manager apps include 1Password, Clipperz, eWallet, KeePass, and LastPass.

Using Remote Access

A paperless office allows greater mobility. If you need a reliable and secure means of accessing your office computer, there are various options for connecting remotely. Some involve hardware and some involve software. One hardware option is the Microsoft Small Business Server, which can provide remote access to your office network through any web browser. Software options include LogMeIn and GoToMyPC, which can be used even if you have Microsoft Small Business Server. Both offer a variety of features, such as file sync and transfer, remote printing, and apps for your smartphone or tablet.

LogMeIn is reliable, cost-effective, and easy to use. This software, coupled with a paperless office, has allowed Donna to retain a valuable employee who remained at home following the births of her children. She logs in to her office computer from her house and works as easily and efficiently as if she were sitting at a desk in the office. Although the free version works well for occasional use, the Pro version is needed for access to important premium features such as file transfer, remote printing, and desktop sharing. An annual subscription for the Pro version is approximately $70 per computer, with discounts available for multiple computers. There is a free app available that makes logging in simple. See the description of LogMeIn Ignition in Lesson 8.

Creating Acrobat Portfolios for Client Documents

Donna's procedures for providing draft documents to clients for review changed significantly as a result of going paperless. Her firm uses Adobe

Acrobat to put together a secure password-protected portfolio of documents. Donna has created a custom "cover page" displaying the firm logo (see Figure 7.1). It is saved as a read-only file on the firm's server so the original remains intact.

Figure 7.1 PDF Portfolio Sample Cover Page

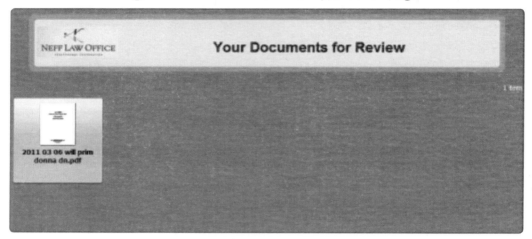

Once the portfolio template is opened and saved with a new name to the client's file, the PDF documents to be shared with the client are added. A "draft" watermark applied to each document will only appear if the document is printed. This helps discourage clients from signing documents that must be printed and signed with witnesses present.

Various security features, including encryption and password protection, are applied to the portfolio before it is e-mailed. The client is provided with the password at the initial meeting. Editing of the documents in the portfolio is restricted by assigning a special internal-use-only password that must be supplied before any editing can be done. (The portfolio permission can be set to allow documents to be printed, since many clients, especially older ones, prefer reviewing paper drafts. Vision problems can make it difficult to review documents onscreen.)

The completed portfolio is attached to an e-mail and sent to the client. The e-mail describes how to download the free Adobe Reader if the client doesn't already have it and what to do if a password is forgotten. Most of Donna's clients prefer to receive documents in this manner, and she loves that documents can be provided quickly and securely to clients ahead of time without the added costs of photocopying and mailing.

To create portfolios using the current version of Adobe Acrobat Pro XI, follow these four simple steps:

1. Choose *File*, select *Create*, and then select *PDF Portfolio*.
2. Choose a layout or choose *Import Custom Layout*.
3. Click *Add Files* and select files you want to share in the portfolio.
4. Rearrange files as desired and click *Finish*.

Undertstanding Digital versus Electronic Signatures

As offices continue to move away from the conventional paper-based way of working, electronic or digital signatures will replace traditional hand-written signatures. A digital signature can provide assurances as to the validity of the document and the identity of who signed it.

To fine-tune your paperless office, you will want to create an electronic or a digital signature in some form. Just what is the difference between an electronic and a digital signature? An electronic signature is essentially a picture of your signature.

A digital signature is a complicated algorithm with public and private keys. It provides authentication and encryption benefits that are impossible with an electronic signature. Basically, when you place a digital signature at the bottom of an e-mail, your recipients know that the content of the e-mail remained completely private during transmission and that it came from your e-mail address. Several third-party providers offer digital signatures.

One thing to note about creating an electronic signature: if you use a smartphone or a tablet to sign documents, you may find it easier to download one of the signing apps mentioned in Lesson 8.

Creating an Electronic Signature in Word

This is a relatively straightforward process with one tricky bit. We'll get into the specifics below, but basically you scan your signature, create a graphic, and then insert that graphic in almost any electronic document that is usually signed. The tricky bit is making your signature graphic appear transparent so it looks as if you signed on the signature line rather than pasting the graphic on top. To see the difference, compare the two signatures in Figure 7.2. The upper signature is not transparent; the lower one is.

Figure 7.2 Nontransparent and Transparent Electronic Signatures

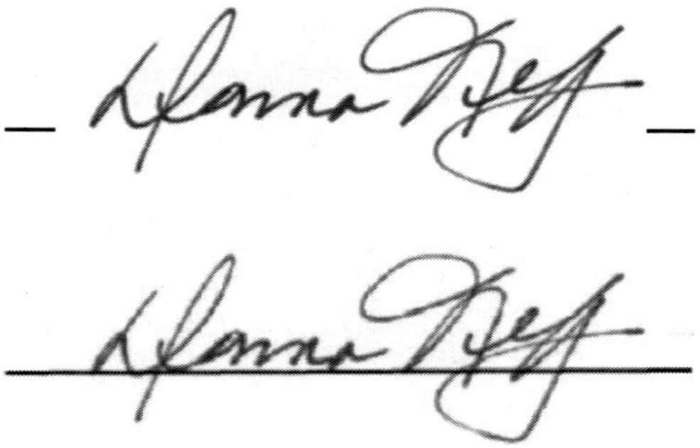

You can make a signature graphic transparent with software like Adobe Photoshop or Photoshop Elements. If you don't have this type of software, you can achieve a similar effect using a feature in Word. It won't look as good as one created using a true graphics application, but it will allow you to produce a reasonably decent transparent signature.

To create a simple transparent electronic signature for Word documents, follow the steps below for Word 2010. The menu items are similar in Word 2007.

1. Using a black ink pen, such as a Sharpie Extra Fine, sign your usual signature on a clean sheet of heavier-quality white paper, such as twenty-pound bond. (If you want the signature to appear in blue, you can change the color later.)

2. Scan your signature using a high resolution, such as 300 dpi, and output as a TIFF file; the file extension will appear as .tif in the document name.

3. Open a new Word document.

4. Under the **Insert** tab, choose *Picture*. Then select the saved TIFF file. Click on *Insert* to display your scanned signature in the Word document.

5. Locate the **Picture Tools – Format** tab on the far right in the **Size** group, and use the *Crop* tool to remove all extra white space. Drag the little corners in toward your signature until the rectangle enclosing the image is as small as possible without losing any of your signature.

6. Still under the **Picture Tools – Format** tab, in the **Adjust** group, select the drop-down arrow under *Color* to display more choices. Select *Set transparent color* and position the cursor (it changes to a peculiar-looking icon rather like a pen with an arrow tip) inside the rectangle over any white space but away from your signature.

You won't notice a difference other than the cursor reverting to its usual shape.

7. Save this Word document.

8. Create a PDF of the file, whether by printing to PDF or selecting **Create PDF** under the **Acrobat** tab. Name the file when prompted.

You can now copy and paste your new electronic signature into any Word document.

Adding an Electronic Signature to a PDF in Adobe Acrobat XI

There are various ways to add an electronic signature to a PDF document using Adobe Acrobat XI Standard or Pro.

Creating a Simple Electronic Signature

1. To create an image of your signature, first sign a piece of paper, then scan it to PDF, name it, and save it.

2. In Acrobat XI, select the **Sign** pane, choose **I Need to Sign**, and select **Place Signature**.

3. Select **Use an Image** for creating your electronic signature.

4. Browse to the file created in step 1 and click **Accept**.

5. Click on your PDF to place your signature. You can move the signature image if it ends up not exactly where you want it.

6. To permanently merge your signature to the PDF, click **Confirm** to finalize changes. Name the file and click **Save**.

7. Adobe allows you to send the file to others through its EchoSign service, which lets you track the signing process and store the file online. To do so, click *Send Signed Document*.

Creating an Authenticated Digital Signature

A true digital signature uses a certificate-based digital ID and provides a higher level of security than the method outlined above. Once you have created an electronic signature, we recommend you take steps to protect it and ensure that you are the only person to use it. Store it on a password-protected USB stick or password-protect the file if it is stored on a shared server or in a shared folder.

1. If you don't already have one, create a digital ID.

- Go to *Preferences* > *Signatures*.
- Choose *Identities & Trusted Certificates*, then click *More*.
- Select *Digital IDs*, then click the *Add ID* button.
- Choose *A new digital ID I want to create now* and click *Next*.
- Fill in the form (name and e-mail are required) and click *Next*.
- Choose where you want to store your ID, give it a password, then click *Finish*.

2. Register your digital ID.

- Go back to *Preferences* > *Signatures*, then click *More* in *Identities & Trusted Certificates.*
- Select *Digital IDs* in the left-hand sidebar
- Click the *Add ID button* and choose *My existing digital ID from: A file*, then click *Next*.
- Browse to select the digital ID you just created, enter the ID's password, then click *Next* and *Finish*.

3. Sign your document.
    (Note: in Acrobat Reader, the PDF must have been saved with
    Reader Usage Rights enabled in order to sign with a certificate.)

    - Complete your edits before you sign because any subsequent
      changes may invalidate the signature.

    - Go to **Sign** > **Work with Certificates** > **Sign with Certificate**.
      Click **Drag new signature rectangle** on the pop-up menu.

    - Drag your cursor to create a box where you want to place
      the signature.

    - Enter your password in the pop-up box and click **Sign**.

E-faxing

E-faxing, also known as Internet fax, e-mail to fax, and fax to e-mail, uses
e-mail to send and receive faxes over the Internet. Generally, you send a
fax as a PDF or TIFF attachment to an e-mail. Many e-faxing service providers (see below) also offer online storage where you can access your faxes.
Your firm will still have a fax number, and many service providers offer
toll-free numbers.

To send a fax, attach the file to an e-mail with the first part of the
address being the recipient's fax number and the latter being the domain
of the service provider; for example, 613-835-0232@faxitnice.com. The
fax is sent to the recipient's fax machine, and you receive an e-mail confirmation. Depending upon the services you purchase, you may also send
faxes directly from your online account.

E-faxing is convenient, easy to use, and offers many benefits because
you don't need a fax machine, paper, ink, toner, or ongoing maintenance.
However, you will need to establish an account with a service provider.
There are many to choose from, each offering a range of options. Monthly

charges apply for a maximum number of pages sent and received, with additional charges for excess pages during the month. Some sample costs are shown in Figure 7.3.

Figure 7.3 Sample Costs for E-faxing

Efax	$18/month for 150 free pages received (then 10 cents/page) and 150 free pages sent (then 10 cents/page)
Myfax	$10/month for 200 pages received and 100 pages sent (overages are 10 cents/page)
Faxitnice	$9.99/month for 500 pages received or sent (overages are 10 cents/page)
Nextiva	$8.95/month for 500 pages received or sent (overages are 3 cents/page)

Before selecting a service provider, compare plans and features. Pick the provider that makes the most sense for your office and its faxing volume. Take advantage of any free trials, and speak to colleagues about their experiences with e-faxing.

Addressing Practice Areas that Present Special Challenges to a Paperless Office

Some areas of practice are paper intensive, creating special challenges for a paperless office. For example, in the specialized area of construction defect cases, there are voluminous paper records that may require you to keep a hybrid paperless office to maintain documentation of the defects. Even so, there can be advantages in choosing to move to a more paperless environment. If you are new to this practice area, check with a construction defect law office to see what needs to be kept in the original form supplied.

Another area presenting special challenges is criminal defense of incarcerated clients. Though a client may have a client file in the prison, there are likely banker boxes filled with details left with the lawyer for safekeeping or transferred to the lawyer handling any postconviction work.

Within the criminal defense practice area is the highly specialized category of capital defense. When the client is at risk of being executed or spending the remainder of his or her life behind bars, the records must often be kept in paper form.

There might come a day when all documents are electronic and questions of proof are met with a digital record, but until that day arrives, particularly in these specialized areas, you may want to keep your files in paper and be very careful to preserve original documents. (Your jurisdiction probably has some version of ABA Model Rule 1.15 and specifies how long you must retain client property.) If you are new to these practice areas, associate with the specialized bar that handles these cases. You will learn how to run a more efficient practice from it. Again, there will be details of your practice that can be in a paperless state, so you will still find going paperless beneficial.

Avoiding Malpractice with Loss Prevention Resources

If you have a malpractice insurance carrier, review its loss prevention materials. There will likely be helpful information regarding going paperless.

In addition, there are over twenty practice management adviser programs in state bars and law societies throughout the United States and Canada. Check with your local bar association to determine whether there is a practice management adviser available to provide assistance. These advisers can answer questions and supply checklists and forms that can be adapted to your needs in a paperless office. They may direct you to paperless law offices you can visit and lawyers you can contact who have gone through the transition process. See the Resources section for locating practice management advisory services and loss prevention materials.

Some apps for lawyers with paperless practices are in Lesson 8.

Apps for the Paperless Lawyer

This lesson discusses some apps (computer software programs used on smartphones and tablets) that can be helpful to lawyers in a paperless practice. We describe the key features of each app and the reasons why you will want to add it to your toolbox; where possible, we list some similar apps so that you can check out the competition before making a decision. Most apps are available for both Android and Apple devices.

GoodReader

Price: $4.99

Platform: iOS

What It Does: As PDFs are the stuff a paperless office is made of, an app that allows you not only to read but also to annotate PDFs is a must. There are quite a few apps that will do the trick, depending upon the features you need. Our favorite, GoodReader, shown in Figure 8.1, opens both PDF and Word files, but only PDF files can be annotated. Annotate PDFs using typewriter mode, highlighting, underlining, using sticky notes, drawing lines, or arrows, and freehand drawing. Download files from the Internet, from e-mail attachments, or directly from your computer via USB connection or Wi-Fi. Easily sync individual files or entire folders with Dropbox, SkyDrive, SugarSync, and others.

Why You Want It: Without question, going paperless means you will work more and more with PDFs. You need to work with these electronic documents just as you did with paper documents. Choose an app such as GoodReader or another with similar features so you can mark up and share PDFs easily among your devices and the people with whom you collaborate.

Similar Apps: Foxit Mobile PDF, iAnnotate PDF, Adobe Reader, PDF Reader Pro, neu. Annotate, ezPDF Reader, RepliGo Reader, qPDF Notes, PDF Expert, PDFpen

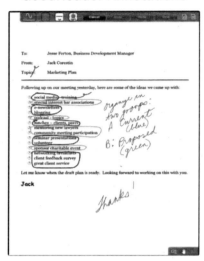

Figure 8.1
GoodReader Annotations

LogMeIn Ignition

Price: $129.99 Works with LogMeIn software on your computer (LogMeIn Free or Pro). iOS, onetime charge; $29.99 Android OS, works with LogMeIn software on your computer (LogMeIn Free or Pro).

Platform: iOS, Android OS

What It Does: This app, which is shown in Figure 8.2, allows you to remotely (and securely) access and control any computer over a Wi-Fi or 3G network, just as if you were sitting in front of that computer. You must first install LogMeIn software (either free or the paid Pro version) on the remote PC and then download LogMeIn Ignition on your iPad or iPhone. LogMeIn Pro comes with added features and is currently about $70 annually. When using the app, you are running software on the remote computer, so compatibility issues are nonexistent, even for proprietary software. If you lose your Internet connection, simply reconnect when it is back, and everything is just where you left it because all applications run on the remote computer, not locally. Some of the many features include file manager for transferring files and saving them to your mobile device; Wake on LAN for remotely waking a sleeping computer; print to Air-Print-compatible printers; video and sound streaming (currently available only for Windows); and integration with popular cloud services such as Dropbox. You can also switch between multiple monitors attached to the remote computer and access a full onscreen keyboard. Some features, such as file transfers and remote printing, are only available if you have the Pro version of LogMeIn installed on the remote computer. Ignition offers additional features over the free app, including HD remote control, access to your files via File Manager and My Cloud Bank, and remote sound.

Figure 8.2 LogMeIn Ignition

Why You Want It: If increased mobility is one of the reasons you are going paperless, this is a tool that truly allows you to work from almost anywhere as if you were still in your office. It's secure, yet firewalls don't get in the way. Three layers of passwords ensure that only you or those you give all of the passwords to can access your computer.

Similar Apps: iTap Mobile RDP, GoToMyPC (the app is free but a paid GoToMyPC subscription is required), iTeleport, iSSH, PocketCloud Remote RDP/VNC

Notability

Price: $0.99

Platform: iPad only

What It Does: Gone are the days when a yellow legal pad was always close at hand, but lawyers' need for note taking has not diminished. We love all the bells and whistles this app has to offer (see Figure 8.3). Draw, integrate, copy, move, style, organize—the features are many. Notes can be shared via e-mail, Dropbox, Box, Twitter, iTunes File Sharing, and AirPrint. One neat option is the ability to automatically link audio recordings to your notes. Simply tap a word in the notes to hear what was being said when you were taking notes. You can also insert web clips, figures, and drawings. Notes can be password protected, and there is an auto-sync backup feature so notes can be automatically uploaded to Dropbox, Box, iDisk, or WebDAV.

Why You Want It: If you want to capture ideas with text, audio, or drawings easily, conveniently, and securely on your device (assuming you don't sync to the cloud), this app is just the thing.

Similar Apps: Note Taker HD (we also use this one), Zoho Notebook, ColorNote, Note Everything, Notes Plus, Penultimate, Notesy

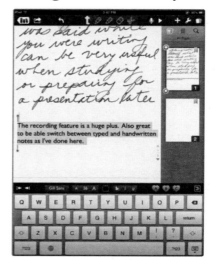

Figure 8.3 Notability

Dictamus

Price: $18.99 (free version very limited but useful for testing the app)

Platform: iOS (an Android version is under development)

What It Does: Whether you dictate a little or a lot, you will want to have a dictation app. Specifically designed for professionals, the Dictamus interface is intuitive and mimics the controls on a physical handheld device (see Figure 8.4). It is very easy to use, and the sound quality is quite impressive. Dictations can be encrypted and sent directly from your device (e-mail, download, FTP, WebDAV, SFTP, Dropbox, Box, etc.). Dictamus offers instant dictation controls, including the ability to move and delete sections in a dictation and easy removal of blank sections of the recording. The free version offers all the features of the paid version, but each dictation is limited to thirty seconds instead of twenty-four hours, and you can only manage five dictations at one time.

Why You Want It: If you frequently use dictation as part of your practice, with Dictamus you can leave your dedicated dictation device at home. One less item to carry is a good thing!

Similar Apps: Dragon Dictation, Philips Dictation Recorder, Voice Dictation, Paper-Port Notes, Winscribe Digital Dictation

Figure 8.4
Dictamus Recorder

Documents To Go Premium (Office Suite)

Price: $17.99 (iOS); $14.99 (Android OS)

Platform: iOS, Android OS

What It Does: As we all encounter Microsoft Word, Excel, and PowerPoint files on a daily basis, an app enabling us to work with these file types is essential. Docs To Go, shown in Figure 8.5, definitely gets a gold star. Effortlessly view, edit, and create Word, Excel, and PowerPoint documents, as well as PDFs. The program allows the original document formatting of edited files to be retained. Features are abundant:

- **Word To Go:** bold, italics, underline, font color, alignment, bullets, tables, bookmarks, comments, footnotes, track changes, word count, find and replace, and more
- **Sheet To Go:** many functions, including formatting (cell, number, and sheet), row and column preferences, AutoFit options, freeze panes, sort, cut, copy, paste, undo, redo, charting, multiple worksheets
- **Slideshow To Go:** edit mode, full screen slide navigations, speaker notes, rehearse timing, and more
- **PDF To Go:** functions include page view, word wrap, Auto-Rotate, bookmarks, search, select and copy text

Figure 8.5
Documents to Go

Store locally or synchronize your documents to the cloud using Google Drive, Dropbox, Box, or SugarSync. These desktop apps allow you to wirelessly move and sync files from your device to your desktop.

Why You Want It: Any app that allows you to work with documents directly is a must-have for the paperless lawyer.

Similar Apps: Quickoffice Pro, Kingsoft Office, OfficeSuite Pro, Smart Office 2

Dropbox

Price: Free (up to 2 GB) or paid (over 2 GB; $9.99 per month and up, depending upon storage needs)

Platform: iOS, Android OS

What It Does: Dropbox (see Figure 8.6) lets you store all your documents, photos, and videos in one place and access them from anywhere on any device or computer. You can earn more space by referring others to the service (500 MB per referral). Additional space can also be purchased per user (Pro) or for a group (Team). Say good-bye to e-mailing attachments back and forth.

Figure 8.6 Dropbox

Simply share a link to a particular document, photo, or video. Once Dropbox is installed on your computer, any file you save to Dropbox will be automatically saved to all your devices, computers, and the Dropbox website. E-mail attachments can be saved straight to your Dropbox. But be aware that there are some security concerns with Dropbox and similar services. You should therefore carefully determine whether they comply with your ethical obligations.

Why You Want It: This app will make your collaborating efforts a breeze.

Similar Apps: Box, SkyDrive, Google Drive, SugarSync, LogMeIn Cubby, Insync, SpiderOak, AVG LiveKive

Evernote

Price: Free (40 MB per month upload; max note size 25 MB) or paid (500 MB per month upload; max note size 50 MB)

Platform: iOS, Android OS

What It Does: Although Evernote (see Figure 8.7) may seem similar to Dropbox, it's not. Dropbox is a file backup and syncing service, but Evernote is for note storing and management as well as syncing. Evernote lets you collect all kinds of information, such as articles, graphics, and video clips, and access them from anywhere you have an Internet connection. You can allow someone to access a notebook directly or just add to it on a notebook-by-notebook basis. Tagging in Evernote is an excellent way to make it easier to find things later, although the search feature is pretty decent too. A search will look not only in notebook titles but also in the notes themselves. A little known feature worth the price of admission is Evernote's ability to apply OCR (convert to digital text) to an image containing text and make it searchable. The image can be from within the Evernote app or from your device's camera. Text must be clear and easily legible. The OCR process happens automatically whenever you add an image to Evernote.

Why You Want It: If you constantly gather information and need somewhere to park it until you can deal with it, work on a variety of platforms (iOS, Windows, Android, and more), and you want to share some of the information, but not all of it, with others, Evernote is just what you need. This app excels at organizing a lot of data in different formats and on a variety of topics.

Similar Apps: Microsoft OneNote, Springpad

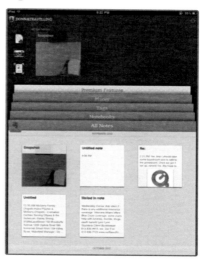

Figure 8.7 Notes in Evernote

TripIt

Price: free (basic features) or $49 per year (TripIt Pro)

Platform: iOS, Android OS

What It Does: If you do any traveling at all, this handy app, shown in Figure 8.8, can eliminate nearly all paper from your travel plans. You won't need paper copies of your itinerary, hotel and car rental details, and so on. TripIt organizes all of that and more in one convenient place accessible via Wi-Fi or 3G networks. If you refresh TripIt before going to an area without Wi-Fi or 3G, all information is available locally on your device. When you receive a confirmation e-mail from a hotel, airline, car rental company, or restaurant, simply forward it to plans@tripit.com from the same e-mail address that you used to create your TripIt account. Extracting information from incoming e-mails, TripIt either adds the details to an existing trip or creates a new trip if there are no matches with dates of existing trips. You can share trip plans with colleagues and family. TripIt Pro comes with additional features such as flight and status alerts, alternative flight info if yours is cancelled, and helpful travel reminders.

Why You Want It: Keeping track of travel plans can be stressful. This app puts all the details in one easy location for instant access and saves paper.

Similar Apps: Kayak, Concur, Travel-Tracker, TripDeck, Easy Travel Planner

Scanner Pro

Price: free or $0.99 (free version has fewer features)

Platform: iOS

What It Does: This app (see Figure 8.9) offers a simple way to turn a paper document into a PDF by either taking a picture with the camera on your device or picking one from your photo album. Snap shots of whiteboards or anything else with text and convert them to something much more useful than simple photographs. Although a device's camera can take photos, it doesn't convert the photos to PDF files. After scanning, the apps show "handles" or "vertex points," which allow you to define what portion of the scan is to be included in the final version. Scanner Pro produces either JPEG or PDF files, which you can then e-mail; upload to Dropbox, Google Drive, Evernote, or

Figure 8.8 TripIt Maps

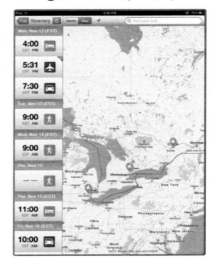

Figure 8.9
Scanner Pro Menu

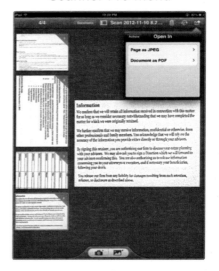

WebDAV; print to an AirPrint-compatible printer; or fax directly from an iPad or iPhone. PDFs can also be password protected.

Why You Want It: As you become a paperless pro, you will try to find ways to avoid carrying or copying paper more and more. With the increased mobility that going paperless allows, you will want to explore ways to capture paper images, convert them to PDF files, and apply OCR to the text. A scanning app is the answer.

Similar Apps: Doc Scan HD, JotNot Scanner Pro (includes OCR feature)

Sign-N-Send

Figure 8.10 Sign-N-Send

Price: $1.99

Platform: iOS

What It Does: This app, shown in Figure 8.10, offers a very simple way to sign PDFs, especially those that arrive as e-mail attachments. Rather than printing, signing, scanning, and sending, simply open the attachment in Sign-N-Send and then, well, sign and send. The app even converts Microsoft Office documents to PDF. Select pen color and size, including highlighters and an eraser. Text can be typed anywhere on the scan in a text box. Export to Dropbox or other apps that work with PDFs.

Why You Want It: As you go paperless, and especially if you become more mobile, you will want to explore the options for signing documents without printing them first.

Similar Apps: SignEasy, SignNow, qPDF Notes, HandySign, DocuSign Ink

LawStack (United States) WiseLii (Canada)

Price: LawStack: free for federal, but fees apply for state codes; WiseLii: free

Platform: iOS

Figure 8.11 LawStack

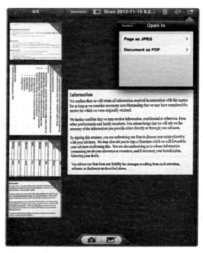

What LawStack Does: LawStack (see Figure 8.11) has been described as a "legal library in your pocket," and there couldn't be a more apt description. Numerous pieces of legislation have been preloaded, such as the US Constitution (as amended May 5, 1992), the Federal Rules of Criminal Procedure, and the Federal Rules of Evidence. You can browse the embedded collection and add items to your stack, including various state codes. Although federal laws are free, state codes must be purchased via links embedded in LawStack. Not all state codes are available yet, but you can request that legislation be added if it isn't there. Other features include offline access, full-text and context-sensitive searches, search highlighting, and bookmarks.

What WiseLii Does: See Figure 8.12 for Canada's equivalent to LawStack, although there are two major differences: legislation for all Canadian provinces and territories is included along with federal legislation, and access to everything is free. You can also search court decisions federally or by province or territory.

Why You Want It: A quick and easy way to conduct basic legal research, especially when you are on the go. Who needs to lug around printed copies of codes and legislation?

Similar Apps: AllLaw, FindLaw, and various state-specific apps

Figure 8.12 WiseLii

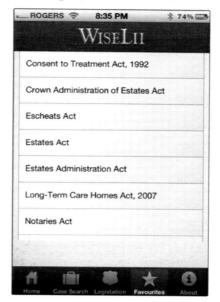

Lesson 9

Ethical Considerations

Because we're talking about information pertaining to clients and their legal matters, to go paperless you must first verify how your jurisdiction views maintaining paperless files; entrusting client information to third-party storage, cloud, or Internet-based storage; and file retention and file destruction. You must also verify what duties of disclosure you have to your client and what informed consent may be required from your client. The ABA Legal Technology Resource Center has compiled cloud ethics opinions from around the United States; see the Resources section for the link.

You will definitely want to address the paperless nature of your office up front with your clients before an engagement letter and fee agreement are signed. Give clients information about safeguards your firm has created to secure client data from unauthorized access and unintended destruction. Many clients may still assume that their files are stored at the office, likely in a paper format in a secure file room. Your duty to communicate everything that is material to your client's case includes advising your client that you maintain a paperless practice and that the client file is maintained in a digital format. The client should know where the file is stored and how it is protected (preferably stored on the firm's server at the office as well as in a password-protected, encrypted format on a third-party storage site that has Department of Defense standards in place for protecting the data).

Would you like clients to complain—with justification—that they weren't told that their personal data was stored on the Internet, and now the storage site has been hacked and their financial information is being sold to identity thieves? This is not as farfetched as you might think. Ensure that this complaint never comes from one of your clients!

Review your jurisdiction's formal ethics opinions. They will give guidance on what is deemed ethical behavior and what is deemed a violation of ethical standards. If there is a website with all the ethics opinions listed, you should look there first. If you don't see a specific opinion addressing the issue, your best option may be to call your jurisdiction's ethics counsel and inquire about ethics opinions pertaining to going paperless and storing or backing up client files on third-party online storage sites.

Your jurisdiction's Rules of Professional Conduct and its ethic opinions should guide you in how you approach this process.

In Canada, the Federation of Law Societies of Canada has adopted a Model Code of Professional Conduct, and although each law society has its own code of conduct, the Federation's Model Code is projected to become the standard over time. In the United States, except for California, state jurisdictions have adopted rules influenced by or adapted from the ABA Model Rules of Professional Conduct and their Comments. Let's look at the ABA Model Rules and Comments (August 2012) and the Federation of Law Societies of Canada Model Code of Professional Conduct and Commentary (December 2012) that are relevant.

ABA Model Rule 1.0: Terminology. (n) "Writing" or "written" denotes a tangible or electronic record of a communication or representation, including handwriting, typewriting, printing, photostating, photography, audio or videorecording, and electronic communications. A "signed" writing includes an electronic sound, symbol or process attached to or logically associated with a writing and executed or adopted by a person with the intent to sign the writing.

Tips: This rule was amended to include electronic communications, which broadens "writing" or "written" to include e-mail and other electronic communications between lawyer and client. This is especially helpful when needing agreement on a fee or a written consent to act, because a client can quickly communicate his or her wishes by e-mail.

ABA Model Rule 1.1: Competence. A lawyer shall provide competent representation to a client. Competent representation requires the legal knowledge, skill, thoroughness and preparation reasonably necessary for the representation.

- **Comment [8]: Maintaining Competence.** To maintain the requisite knowledge and skill, a lawyer should keep abreast of changes in the law and its practice, including the benefits and risks associated with relevant technology, engage in continuing study and education and comply with all continuing legal education requirements to which the lawyer is subject.

Federation Model Code 3.1: Competence. 3.1-1: "Competent lawyer" means a lawyer who has and applies relevant knowledge, skills and attributes in a manner appropriate to each matter undertaken on behalf of a client and the nature and terms of the lawyer's engagement, including:

(i)   managing one's practice effectively;

(k)   otherwise adapting to changing professional requirements, standards, techniques, and practices.

Federation Model Code 3.1: Competence. 3.1-2: A lawyer must perform all legal services undertaken on a client's behalf to the standard of a competent lawyer.

Tips: There is no excuse for delivering incompetent legal services because you don't understand the technology. Test computer backups by periodically conducting a restore of the backup data. Check scans before shredding the original documents. If you are unsure about the technology, learn how to use it. Have an office "cookbook" that explains how to do everything from changing the postage in the postage machine to saving scanned documents into the proper subdirectory on the server. Don't let there be only one person who knows how to do e-filing, since that person may be sick on the very day when you need something filed at court and the deadline has arrived.

ABA Model Rule 1.4: Communication. (a) A lawyer shall: . . .

(3) keep the client reasonably informed about the status of the matter

(4) promptly comply with reasonable requests for information.

- **Comment [4]: Communicating with Client.** A lawyer's regular communication with clients will minimize the occasions on which a client will need to request information concerning the representation. When a client makes a reasonable request for information, however, paragraph (a)(4) requires prompt compliance with the request, or if a prompt response is not feasible, that the lawyer, or a member of the lawyer's staff, acknowledge receipt of the request and advise the client when a response may be expected. A lawyer should promptly respond to or acknowledge client communications.

Federation Model Code 3.2: Quality of Service. 3.2-2: When advising a client, a lawyer must be honest and candid and must inform the client of all information known to the lawyer that may affect the interests of the client in the matter.

Tips: Make use of virtual receptionists to ensure you receive messages from your clients. Respond to calls and e-mails within forty-eight hours, if not twenty-four. Use helpful forms to transmit brief client updates and status reports. Conduct weekly work-in-progress (WIP) meetings with staff, and assign someone to fill out status updates for respective clients.

ABA Model Rule 1.6: Confidentiality of Information. (a) A lawyer shall not reveal information relating to the representation of a client unless the client gives informed consent, the disclosure is impliedly authorized in order to carry out the representation, or the disclosure is permitted by paragraph (b).

> **(b)** A lawyer may reveal information relating to the representation of a client to the extent the lawyer reasonably believes necessary: . . . (6) to comply with other law or a court order; or **(7)** to detect and resolve conflicts of interest arising from the lawyer's change of employment or from changes in the composition or ownership of a firm, but only if the revealed information would not compromise the attorney-client privilege or otherwise prejudice the client.

> **(c)** A lawyer shall make reasonable efforts to prevent the inadvertent or unauthorized disclosure of, or unauthorized access to, information relating to the representation of a client.

Comment [18] Acting Competently to Preserve Confidentiality.
Paragraph (c) requires a lawyer to act competently to safeguard information relating to the representation of a client against . . . unauthorized disclosure by the lawyer or other persons who are participating in the representation of the client or who are subject to the lawyer's supervision. See Rules 1.1, 5.1, and 5.3. The unauthorized access to, or the inadvertent or unauthorized disclosure of, information relating to the representation of a client does not constitute a violation of paragraph (c) if the lawyer has made reasonable efforts to prevent the access or disclosure. Factors to be considered in determining the reasonableness of the lawyer's efforts include, but are not limited to, the sensitivity of the information, the likelihood of disclosure if additional safeguards are not employed, the

cost of employing additional safeguards, the difficulty of implementing the safeguards, and the extent to which the safeguards adversely affect the lawyer's ability to represent clients (e.g., by making a device or important piece of software excessively difficult to use). A client may require the lawyer to implement special security measures not required by this Rule or may give informed consent to forgo security measures that would otherwise be required by this Rule. Whether a lawyer may be required to take additional steps to safeguard a client's information in order to comply with other law, such as state and federal laws that govern data privacy or that impose notification requirements upon the loss of, or unauthorized access to, electronic information, is beyond the scope of these Rules. For a lawyer's duties when sharing information with nonlawyers outside the lawyer's own firm, see Rule 5.3, Comments [3]-[4].

Federation Model Code 3.3: Confidentiality. 3.3-1: A lawyer at all times must hold in strict confidence all information concerning the business and affairs of a client acquired in the course of the professional relationship and must not divulge any such information unless: **(a)** expressly or impliedly authorized by the client; **(b)** required by law or a court to do so; **(c)** required to deliver the information to the Law Society; or **(d)** otherwise permitted by this rule.

- **Commentary [9].** In some situations, the authority of the client to disclose may be inferred. For example, in court proceedings some disclosure may be necessary in a pleading or other court document. Also, it is implied that a lawyer may, unless the client directs otherwise, disclose the client's affairs to partners and associates in the law firm and, to the extent necessary, to administrative staff and to others whose services are used by the lawyer. But this implied authority to disclose places the lawyer under a duty to impress upon associates, employees, students, and other lawyers engaged under contract with the lawyer or with the firm of the lawyer the importance of non-disclosure (both during their employment and afterwards) and require the lawyer to take reasonable care to prevent their disclosing or using any information that the lawyer is bound to keep in confidence.

Tips: Ensure client files are properly shredded. It is your responsibility to safeguard personal identification information. Use proper secure passwords on smartphones so that if a phone is lost, client data is not accessible by third parties. Because of the evolving views of ethics commentators, you should address confidentiality issues with clients before sending e-mails. Discourage clients from reviewing legal e-mail on their work computers. Read the terms of service and privacy statements of online providers. Use confidentiality agreements with staff and vendors.

ABA Model Rule 1.9: Duties to Former Clients. (c) A lawyer who has formerly represented a client in a matter or whose present or former firm has formerly represented a client in a matter shall not thereafter: . . .**(2)** reveal information relating to the representation except as these Rules would permit or require with respect to a client.

Federation Model Code 3.3: Confidentiality. 3.3-1: A lawyer at all times must hold in strict confidence all information concerning the business and affairs of a client acquired in the course of the professional relationship and must not divulge any such information unless: **(a)** expressly or impliedly authorized by the client; **(b)** required by law or a court to do so; **(c)** required to deliver the information to the Law Society; or **(d)** otherwise permitted by this rule.

- **Commentary [3].** A lawyer owes the duty of confidentiality to every client without exception and whether or not the client is a continuing or casual client. The duty survives the professional relationship and continues indefinitely after the lawyer has ceased to act for the client, whether or not differences have arisen between them.

Tips: Assuming you retain paper records until an engagement is completed, be careful to shred client files when the file retention guideline period is over. Store printed client files in a safe, secure storage area. Keep proper records of what is in your storage facility. Make arrangements for timely file destruction so that you do not incur a storage bill that you are unable to pay in the future. If there is no reason to keep a copy of a client file beyond ten years, it becomes a ballooning liability if you keep it for thirty years. Some public storage facilities will refuse to allow you to access your stored items if you have fallen behind on payments. More troubling is the fact that a facility's policy may be to auction contents of storage units if rent is not paid. Your client materials and the information they contain could be auctioned off along with the extra office equipment in storage.

ABA Model Rule 1.15: Safekeeping Property. (a) A lawyer shall hold property of clients or third persons that is in a lawyer's possession in connection with a representation separate from the lawyer's own property. . . . Other property shall be identified as such and appropriately safeguarded. Complete records of such account funds and other property shall be kept by the lawyer and shall be preserved for a period of [five years] after termination of the representation.

Federation Model Code 3.5: Preservation of Clients' Property. 3.5-1: In this rule, "property" includes a client's money, securities as defined in [provincial legislation], original documents such as wills, title deeds, minute books, licences, certificates and the like, and all other papers such as client's correspondence, files, reports, invoices and other such documents, as well as personal property including precious and semi-precious metals, jewelry and the like. **3.5-2:** A lawyer must: **(a)** care for a client's property as a careful and prudent owner would when dealing with like property; and **(b)** observe all relevant rules and law about the preservation of a client's property entrusted to a lawyer.

Tips: Check with your local ethics rules for the period of storage time required. Create a client file inventory as client files are closed. Return property to clients at the termination of a client matter, if not sooner. If you use online banking services, make copies of bank statements and reconciliations of trust account(s) either by printing out hard copies or by printing to PDF (to create a digital record) and backing it up. Most online banking records are only accessible for two years. You may be in violation of your ethics rules if you don't preserve the records for the entire time required.

The first sentence in Comment [1] to Model Rule 1.15 discusses the standard for holding property of others: "A lawyer should hold property of others with the care required of a professional fiduciary." This is a very high standard. Bank statements should be reconciled with your trust account(s) monthly to assure that each client's money is properly accounted for. Be sure to use trust accounting software or learn how to properly handle trust accounting by using client ledger cards (paper or electronic), a trust journal (equivalent to a checkbook register), and a monthly reconciliation form to balance the individual sub-accounts to your trust accounts and to the reconciled trust account bank statement.

ABA Model Rule 1.16: Declining or Terminating Representation. (d) Upon

termination of representation, a lawyer shall take steps to the extent reasonably practicable to protect a client's interests, such as giving reasonable notice to the client, allowing time for employment of other counsel, surrendering papers and property to which the client is entitled and refunding any advance payment of fee or expense that has not been earned or incurred. The lawyer may retain papers relating to the client to the extent permitted by other law.

Federation Model Code 3.7: Withdrawal from Representation. 3.7-9:
On discharge or withdrawal, a lawyer must: **(b)** subject to the lawyer's right to a lien, deliver to or to the order of the client all papers and property to which the client is entitled; **(c)** subject to any applicable trust conditions, give the client all relevant information in connection with the case or matter; **(d)** account for all funds of the client then held or previously dealt with, including the refunding of any remuneration not earned during the representation; **(e)** promptly render an account for outstanding fees and disbursements; **(f)** cooperate with the successor lawyer in the transfer of the file so as to minimize expense and avoid prejudice to the client.

Tips: Ensure that the client file records, including trust account records, are updated on a timely basis so that should either party terminate the representation, you can quickly provide all of the records the client is entitled to receive. A delay in getting file documents is disturbing to a client, especially when the lawyer has been fired.

ABA Model Rule 1.18: Duties to Prospective Client. (b) Even when no client-lawyer relationship ensues, a lawyer who has learned information from a prospective client shall not use or reveal that information, except as Rule 1.9 would permit with respect to information of a former client.

- **Comment [3].** It is often necessary for a prospective client to reveal information to the lawyer during an initial consultation prior to the decision about formation of a client-lawyer relationship. The lawyer often must learn such information to determine whether there is a conflict of interest with an existing client and whether the matter is one that the lawyer is willing to undertake. Paragraph (b) prohibits the lawyer from using or revealing that information, except as permitted by Rule 1.9, even if the client or lawyer decides not to proceed with the representation. The duty exists regardless of how brief the initial conference may be.

Federation Model Code 3.3: Confidentiality. 3.3-1: A lawyer at all times must hold in strict confidence all information concerning the business and affairs of a client acquired in the course of the professional relation-ship and must not divulge any such information unless: **(a)** expressly or impliedly authorized by the client; **(b)** required by law or a court to do so; **(c)** required to deliver the information to the Law Society; or **(d)** other-wise permitted by this rule.

- **Commentary [4].** A lawyer also owes a duty of confidentiality to anyone seeking advice or assistance on a matter invoking a law-yer's professional knowledge, although the lawyer may not render an account or agree to represent that person. A solicitor and client relationship is often established without formality. A lawyer should be cautious in accepting confidential information on an informal or preliminary basis, since possession of the information may prevent the lawyer from subsequently acting for another party in the same or a related matter (see rule 3.4-1: Conflicts).

Tips: Ensure confidentiality of the client data you have gathered. Properly shred personally identifying information.

ABA Model Rule 5.1: Responsibilities of Partners, Managers, and Super-visory Lawyers. (c) A lawyer shall be responsible for another lawyer's violation of the Rules of Professional Conduct if: **(1)** the lawyer orders or, with knowledge of the specific conduct, ratifies the conduct involved; or **(2)** the lawyer is a partner or has comparable managerial authority in the law firm in which the other lawyer practices, or has direct supervisory authority over the other lawyer, and knows of the conduct at a time when its consequences can be avoided or mitigated but fails to take reasonable remedial action.

Tips: Although you may delegate details of going paperless to others, remember the famous words of President Truman: "The buck stops here."

You are responsible. Ensure that the policy at your law firm complies with the ethical rules and that the policy is followed.

ABA Model Rule 5.2: Responsibilities of a Subordinate Lawyer. (a)

A lawyer is bound by the Rules of Professional Conduct notwithstanding that the lawyer acted at the direction of another person.

Tips: Know the ethical rules that apply and point out potential violations to your supervising lawyer. Will you get fired for refusing to act in a way that would result in breaking a rule of professional conduct? Seek ethics advice.

ABA Model Rule 5.3: Responsibilities Regarding Nonlawyer Assistance.

With respect to a nonlawyer employed or retained by or associated with a lawyer: . . . **(c)** a lawyer shall be responsible for conduct of such a person that would be a violation of the Rules of Professional Conduct if engaged in by a lawyer if: **(1)** the lawyer orders or, with the knowledge of the specific conduct, ratifies the conduct involved; or **(2)** the lawyer is a partner or has comparable managerial authority in the law firm in which the person is employed, or has direct supervisory authority over the person, and knows of the conduct at a time when its consequences can be avoided or mitigated but fails to take reasonable remedial action.

Federation Model Code 6.1: Supervision. 6.1-1: A lawyer has complete professional responsibility for all business entrusted to him or her and must directly supervise staff and assistants to whom the lawyer delegates particular tasks and functions.

- **Commentary [1].** A lawyer may permit a non-lawyer to act only under the supervision of a lawyer. The extent of supervision will depend on the type of legal matter, including the degree of standardization and repetitiveness of the matter, and the experience of the non-lawyer generally and with regard to the matter in question. The burden rests on the lawyer to educate a non-lawyer concerning the duties that the lawyer assigns to the non-lawyer and then to supervise the manner in which such duties are carried out. A lawyer should review the non-lawyer's work at sufficiently frequent intervals to enable the lawyer to ensure its proper and timely completion

Tips: If your cloud service provider has a breach, does it notify all clients? If the courier service leaves your client file in an unlocked vehicle and it is stolen, are you notified? Read the terms of service and privacy statement of any third party you entrust with confidential information. Properly train your support staff so that they understand the importance of compliance with ethical rules such as confidentiality and protection of client property. Ensure compliance with the protocols and safeguards that you adopt at your law office.

Conclusion

What Lies Ahead

Let's face it: we are pioneers. One of Sheila's favorite props when speaking about technology is a collection of storage discs: from those big square floppies to small hard plastic discs to CDs to USB thumb drives. What drives home the point is that these items all were given as CLE materials from her state bar association over a period spanning less than ten years! We have come so far; now CLE materials are likely to be available on an app or as a download from a website.

You may feel positively ancient when you recall using the fancy and enormous word processing machines from the early 1980s. Do you remember DOS? Do you remember the first "brick" cell phones? Perhaps you laughed at someone who suggested biometric scanning could be used to restrict access to a computer, thinking it was too much like a James Bond movie to ever happen. We have indeed come far, and quickly.

Technology continues to advance at breakneck speed. It enabled the authors to use Dropbox to collaborate and facilitate the writing and organization of this book and its peer review. With Donna in Ottawa, Ontario, and Sheila in Portland, Oregon, both of us felt far closer when one would be at her computer and see a notice that the other had just uploaded a revised chapter. Separated by 2,647 miles, we could immediately check each other's revisions with a click.

Without a doubt, people will soon have more immediate access to one another via smarter phones, smaller tablets, and speedier computers. Technology allows us to do more for less money, and do so faster. Looking back at how far we've come, it's hard to imagine just where we will go next.

What platform you use in your law office is increasingly unimportant. It seems very plausible that we will have more SaaS and have our applications hosted by providers that are regional or national. Do we need more capacity on a laptop or computer? Or just faster access to the Internet and backup relays so if one access goes down, our computer switches seamlessly to another relay or Internet service broker? The big push for innovation will likely continue to come from clients who want faster and more affordable access to the highest level of legal services. With far-flung legal teams, paperless offices support lawyers and their clients in sharing digital data and electronic documents. What we might have thought nearly impossible just a short time ago is now reality—and then some. Whatever changes technology does bring, we need to do our best to at least stay current. Our clients expect no less.

Resources

We think that providing legal services to clients in a paperless manner is a worthwhile and attainable goal. Because our purpose in this book was to provide you with a quick read on the topic, we have listed several resources for you to explore further, but there are still many left to discover. Be sure to add some lines after each category so that readers can jot down their own favorites. Please share your resources with us so we can share them with others. We'll give you credit for any suggestions!

Books

Cloud Computing for Lawyers, by Nicole Black. ABA LPM Section, 2012. http://apps.americanbar.org/abastore/index.cfm?section=main&fm=Product.AddToCart&pid=5110724.

iPad Apps in One Hour for Lawyers, by Tom Mighell. ABA LPM Section, 2012. http://apps.americanbar.org/abastore/index.cfm?section=-main&fm=Product.AddToCart&pid=5110739.

iPad at Work, by David Sparks. Wiley, 2011.

iPad in One Hour for Lawyers, by Tom Mighell. 2nd ed. ABA LPM Section, 2012. http://apps.americanbar.org/abastore/index.cfm?section=-main&fm=Product.AddToCart&pid=5110747.

iPad 2 Secrets, by Mark Errett, Tom Oxlade, and Jon Bonnick. Intelligenti Ltd., 2011.

Practice Law in the Cloud, by David Whelan. Carswell Thomson Reuters, 2012.

Virtual Law Practice: How to Deliver Legal Services Online, by Stephanie L. Kimbro. ABA LPM Section, 2010. http://apps.americanbar.org/abastore/index.cfm?section=main&fm=Product.AddToCart&pid=5110707.

Blogs

eLawyering Blog, by Richard S. Granat. http://www.elawyeringredux.com/.

Virtual Law Practice, by Stephanie L. Kimbro. http://virtuallawpractice.org/.

Publications

"eLawyering for a Competitive Advantage: How to Earn Legal Fees While You Sleep," by Richard S. Granat. 2008. http://meetings.abanet.org/webupload/commupload/EP024500/fsrelatedresources/eLawyering_for_Competitive_Advantage.pdf.

"Guidelines for the Use of Cloud Computing in Law Practice," eLawyering Task Force, ABA LPM Section. 2011. http://meetings.abanet.org/webupload/commupload/EP024500/relatedresources/cloudcomputingguidelines05.30.2011.pdf.

Law Practice, virtual practice issue, September/October 2011. ABA LPM Section. http://www.americanbar.org/publications/law_practice_magazine/2011/september_october.html.

Law Practice Today, paperless office issue, September 2009. ABA LPM Section. http://www.americanbar.org/publications/law_practice_today_home/law_practice_today_archive/september09.html.

Law Practice Today, Special Edition: Disaster Law–Preparing Law Firms and Clients for Issues in Cyberspace, March 2012. ABA LPM Section.

http://www.americanbar.org/publications/law_practice_today_home/law_practice_today_archive/march12.html.

Law Practice Today, working remotely issue, June 2009. ABA LPM Section. http://www.americanbar.org/publications/law_practice_today_home/law_practice_today_archive/june09.html.

Law Practice Today, cloud issue, May 2012. ABA LPM Section. http://www.americanbar.org/publications/law_practice_today_home/law_practice_today_archive/may12.html.

"Managing the Security and Privacy of Electronic Data in a Law Office," PracticePRO. 2005. http://www.americanbar.org/content/dam/aba/administrative/lawyers_professional_liability/managingsecurityprivacy-4print.authcheckdam.pdf.

"The Paperless Office," by Donna Neff. *Ontario Lawyers' Gazette*, Summer 2009. http://www.lsuc.on.ca/media/olg_summer09_paperless.pdf.

"Suggested Minimum Requirement for Law Firms Delivering Services Online," eLawyering Task Force, ABA LPM Section. 2009. (for discussion at time of publication) http://meetings.abanet.org/webupload/commupload/EP024500/relatedresources/Minimum_Requirements_for_Lawyers_2009_10_24.pdf.

"Tips and Tricks for Developing a Document Management System," by Donna Neff and Natalie Sanna. AB*A Law Practice Today*, January 2010. http://www.abanet.org/lpm/lpt/articles/ftr01105.shtml.

Websites

ABA eLawyering Task Force, http://apps.americanbar.org/dch/committee.cfm?com=EP024500

ABA Law Practice Division : Practice Management Advisors/State and Local Bar Outreach Committee, http://apps.americanbar.org/dch/committee.cfm?com=EP024000&edit=1.

ABA Legal Technology Resource Center, http://www.americanbar.org/groups/departments_offices/legal_technology_resources.html.

"Cloud Computing/Software as a Service for Lawyers," ABA Legal Technology Resource Center, http://www.americanbar.org/groups/departments_offices/legal_technology_resources/resources/charts_fyis/saas.html.

"Cloud Ethics Opinions Around the U.S.," ABA Legal Technology Resource Center, http://www.americanbar.org/groups/departments_offices/legal_technology_resources/resources/charts_fyis/cloud-ethics-chart.html.

"FYI: Playing It Safe with Encryption," ABA Legal Technology Resource Center, http://www.americanbar.org/groups/departments_offices/legal_technology_resources/resources/charts_fyis/FYI_Playing_it_safe.html.

Appendix

File Naming

What's in a Name?

Every electronic document, once scanned or printed to PDF, must be named in a standardized, consistent manner so users can identify, locate, and sort documents quickly and easily. The file name should contain just enough details so that any team member knows what a document is without having to open it.

Donna Neff's File-Naming Protocols

Here is a sample file name showing the common components that we use in our system followed by an explanation of each component.

2011 02 04 let report re deed SENT rn.pdf

Table A.1 The Components of a File Name

Component	Explanation
2011 02 04	• keep in mind how files will be sorted within a folder or sub-folder • we use the date on which file was originally created • specific format: 4-digit year, 2-digit month, and 2-digit day • format allows all files within a folder to be sorted chronologically
let	• abbreviation indicating the type of document, e.g., let for letter, eml for email, t-c for notes about a telephone call
report re	• brief description of the contents of the document • the least structured component; risk of being too wordy • encourage very short descriptions (2 or 3 words) • various unwritten standard practices will develop over time
SENT	• differentiate between received and sent documents; for example, 'SENT' is included in the file name for all documents that have left our office by whatever means (fax, email, paper mail, etc.)
rn	• initials of the person who created the file • in case questions arise later
Warranty/Returns	• 90-day minimum money-back guarantee • Watch for restocking fees • Minimum 2-3 years parts and labor coverage • Tip: Ensure backlight and multiple pixel defects are covered by warranty.

Tracking Versions

Document Management Systems track different versions of a document. The first draft of a document is named and in subsequent drafts, the document name includes a revision numbers. In Donna's firm, the initials of the second team member to review or revise the document are added. If revised several times, revision numbers are also added to the initials of the person revising. Obviously this will not be workable if there are six or seven people working on the document as the name will become cumbersome.

How a File Name Changes in Donna's Office

Table A.2 shows how a file name would change throughout the development of a document at Donna's office. In this example, a Will is being drafted for a client and the Will file name changes at each stage of the drafting and review process. This system is workable in a small office. If a number of people review and revise a document, the name would get unwieldy.

Table A.2

First draft created by law clerk	2009 08 26 Will H ds.docx
Draft reviewed by lawyer	2009 08 26 Will H ds-rn.docx
Draft further revised by law clerk	2009 08 26 Will H ds2-rn.docx
Drafted further revised and finalized by lawyer	2009 08 26 Will H ds2-rn2.docx

For different types of documents, consider the key information that you want included. For example, when naming files for brochures, forms, and the like, Donna's office omits the date and includes only the version number before the team member's initials, if any. For such materials, the firm decided that the version number, and not the original creation date, is important to track.

Dan Siegel's File-Naming Protocols

Before implementing a File Naming Protocol, it is important to have a directory structure and substructure in order for files to be located in the appropriate directories rather than willy-nilly or in one large directory.

Thus, many firms have separate directories for client files and firm business files, with each client filed divided into subdirectories.

There are many possible file naming and directory naming protocols. First, consider the following suggested directory names:

- **COR**   Correspondence, Letters, Faxes & Email
- **EXP**   Expenses & Bills
- **MED**   Medical Records
- **MEM**   Memoranda, Notes, Research, Interview Records, Fee Agreements, HIPAA Authorizations, etc.
- **PLD**   Pleadings & Discovery (Some firms use a DISC directory for discovery)
- **TRL**   Trial & Pre-Trial-Related Documents

Thus, the file structure for firm adopting this protocol would appear as in Figure A.3:

Figure A.3 Client File Structure with Sub-Folders

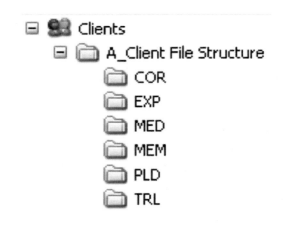

Dates

In addition, when naming files, dates should *always* be entered YEAR-MONTH-DATE (XXXX-YY-ZZ) (*e.g.,* 2006-12-25) so that similarly named documents will sort numerically in date order. If dates are listed in any other manner, they will not sort properly chronologically.

Suggested File Naming Protocols

A File Naming Protocol should reflect how your office operates and, when possible, use universally understood naming conventions. These examples are intended as a starting point, and should be adapted to each firm's specific needs.

COR Directory

Letters from the firm should be saved as:

- Ltr to <u>Name</u> <u>Date</u> <u>Subject</u>

  e.g., Ltr to Atty Scott 2005-01-25 With Doc Requests

Letters to the firm should be saved as:

- Ltr from <u>Name</u> <u>Date</u> <u>Subject</u>

  e.g., Ltr from Atty Scott 2005-01-25 With Doc Requests

Faxes should be saved as:

- Fax to <u>Name</u> <u>Date</u> <u>Subject</u>
- Fax from <u>Name</u> <u>Date</u> <u>Subject</u>

Email should be saved as:

- Email to <u>Name</u> <u>Date</u> <u>Subject</u>
- Email from <u>Name</u> <u>Date</u> <u>Subject</u>

MEM Directory

Memos from the firm

- Memo to <u>Name</u> <u>Date</u> <u>Subject</u>

    e.g., Memo to JDF 2001-05-25 re Expert Witness

PLD Directory

Documents in this directory should be named based upon the type of document/filing – or the response to the document/filing – and the dated created/filed, such as:

- Complaint – Answer of <u>Party</u> Filed <u>Date</u>
- Complaint (Amended) – Filed <u>Date</u>
- Complaint Filed <u>Date</u>
- Complaint – Answer of <u>Party</u> to New Matter of <u>Party</u> Filed <u>Date</u>
- Interrogatories (Set XX) of <u>Party</u> 2005-01-10
- Interrogatories (Set XX) of <u>Party</u> – Answer of <u>Party</u> <u>Date</u>
- Motion to/for <u>Subject</u> 2005-01-10
- Motion to/for <u>Subject</u> – Answer of <u>Party</u> Filed <u>Date</u>
- Order <u>Subject of Order</u> <u>Date</u>
- Preliminary Objections of <u>Party</u> Filed <u>Date</u>
- Request for Admissions (Set XX) of <u>Party</u> <u>Date</u>
- Request for Production (Set XX) of <u>Party</u> <u>Date</u>

Other pleadings should be similarly named. Generally, do not name documents starting with Plaintiff's, etc., because of the large number of documents that will be named that way.

TRL Directory

This directory should contain only pre-trial documents and documents intended to be used at Trial, including transcripts, depositions, CaseMap summaries, etc. such as:

- Deposition <u>Witness Name</u> Date
- Expert Witness Report of <u>Witness Name</u> for <u>Party</u> <u>Date</u>
- Proposed Jury Interrogatories of <u>Party</u> <u>Date</u>
- Proposed Points for Charge of <u>Party</u> <u>Date</u>
- Transcript <u>Description/Subject</u> <u>Date</u>

MEDS Directory

Name documents based upon the provider's name, with dates of treatment or other identifying information, such as:

- Lankenau Hospital Records, <u>Date(s)</u> In-Patient Hospitalization
- Lankenau Hospital Records, Various Emergency Room Visits
- William Smith, M.D., Treatment Records 2005-2006
- John James, D.O., Office Notes 2005-01-23 to 2006-02-02

REMEMBER...

When naming files, dates should always be entered

YEAR-MONTH-DATE (XXXX-YY-ZZ) (e.g., 2006-12-25)

so that similarly named documents will always sort alphabetically and in date order. If dates are listed in any other manner, they will not sort properly chronologically.

Index

SELECTED BOOKS FROM THE LAW PRACTICE DIVISION

The Lawyer's Guide to Microsoft Outlook 2013
By Dennis Kennedy and Allison C. Shields

Product Code: 5110752 • LP Price: $41.95 • Regular Price: $69.95

Take control of your e-mail, calendar, to-do list, and more with *The Lawyer's Guide to Microsoft® Outlook 2013*. This essential guide summarizes the most important new features in the newest version of Microsoft® Outlook and provides practical tips that will promote organization and productivity in your law practice. Written specifically for lawyers by a twenty-year veteran of law office technology and ABA member, this book will help you:

- Clean up your inbox and organize e-mail messages
- Manage appointments and meetings with your calendar
- Improve efficiency with the Outlook task list
- Track phone calls and time with the journal
- Search for e-mails and attachments
- Access Outlook from web and mobile devices
- Archive materials from old cases
- Troubleshoot when things go wrong
- Avoid Outlook mistakes commonly made by lawyers
- Save time with keyboard shortcuts
- And much more!

Blogging in One Hour for Lawyers
By Ernie Svenson

Product Code: 5110744 • LP Price: $24.95 • Regular Price: $39.95

Until a few years ago, only the largest firms could afford to engage an audience of millions. Now, lawyers in any size firm can reach a global audience at little to no cost—all because of blogs. An effective blog can help you promote your practice, become more "findable" online, and take charge of how you are perceived by clients, journalists and anyone who uses the Internet. Blogging in One Hour for Lawyers will show you how to create, maintain, and improve a legal blog—and gain new business opportunities along the way. In just one hour, you will learn to:

- Set up a blog quickly and easily
- Write blog posts that will attract clients
- Choose from various hosting options like Blogger, TypePad, and WordPress
- Make your blog friendly to search engines, increasing your ranking
- Tweak the design of your blog by adding customized banners and colors
- Easily send notice of your blog posts to Facebook and Twitter
- Monitor your blog's traffic with Google Analytics and other tools
- Avoid ethics problems that may result from having a legal blog

The Electronic Evidence and Discovery Handbook: Forms, Checklists, and Guidelines
By Sharon D. Nelson, Bruce A. Olson, and John W. Simek

Product Code: 5110569 • LP Price: $99.95 • Regular Price: $129.95

The use of electronic evidence has increased dramatically over the past few years, but many lawyers still struggle with the complexities of electronic discovery. This substantial book provides lawyers with the templates they need to frame their discovery requests and provides helpful advice on what they can subpoena. In addition to the ready-made forms, the authors also supply explanations to bring you up to speed on the electronic discovery field. The accompanying CD-ROM features over 70 forms, including, Motions for Protective Orders, Preservation and Spoliation Documents, Motions to Compel, Electronic Evidence Protocol Agreements, Requests for Production, Internet Services Agreements, and more. Also included is a full electronic evidence case digest with over 300 cases detailed!

Facebook® in One Hour for Lawyers
By Dennis Kennedy and Allison C. Shields

Product Code: 5110745 • LP Price: $24.95 • Regular Price: $39.95

With a few simple steps, lawyers can use Facebook® to market their services, grow their practices, and expand their legal network—all by using the same methods they already use to communicate with friends and family. *Facebook® in One Hour for Lawyers* will show any attorney—from Facebook® novices to advanced users—how to use this powerful tool for both professional and personal purposes.

Android Apps in One Hour for Lawyers
By Daniel J. Siegel

Product Code: 5110754 • LP Price: $19.95 • Regular Price: $34.95

Lawyers are already using Android devices to make phone calls, check e-mail, and send text messages. After the addition of several key apps, Android smartphones or tablets can also help run a law practice. From the more than 800,000 apps currently available, Android Apps in One Hour for Lawyers highlights the "best of the best" apps that will allow you to practice law from your mobile device. In just one hour, this book will describe how to buy, install, and update Android apps, and help you:

- Store documents and files in the cloud
- Use security apps to safeguard client data on your phone
- Be organized and productive with apps for to-do lists, calendar, and contacts
- Communicate effectively with calling, text, and e-mail apps
- Create, edit, and organize your documents
- Learn on the go with news, reading, and reference apps
- Download utilities to keep your device running smoothly
- Hit the road with apps for travel
- Have fun with games and social media apps

Virtual Law Practice:
How to Deliver Legal Services Online
By Stephanie L. Kimbro

Product Code: 5110707 • **LP Price:** $47.95 • **Regular Price:** $79.95

The legal market has recently experienced a dramatic shift as lawyers seek out alternative methods of practicing law and providing more affordable legal services. Virtual law practice is revolutionizing the way the public receives legal services and how legal professionals work with clients. If you are interested in this form of practicing law, *Virtual Law Practice* will help you:

- Responsibly deliver legal services online to your clients
- Successfully set up and operate a virtual law office
- Establish a virtual law practice online through a secure, client-specific portal
- Manage and market your virtual law practice
- Understand state ethics and advisory opinions
- Find more flexibility and work/life balance in the legal profession

Social Media for Lawyers: The Next Frontier
By Carolyn Elefant and Nicole Black

Product Code: 5110710 • **LP Price:** $47.95 • **Regular Price:** $79.95

The world of legal marketing has changed with the rise of social media sites such as Linkedin, Twitter, and Facebook. Law firms are seeking their companies attention with tweets, videos, blog posts, pictures, and online content. Social media is fast and delivers news at record pace. This book provides you with a practical, goal-centric approach to using social media in your law practice that will enable you to identify social media platforms and tools that fit your practice and implement them easily, efficiently, and ethically.

iPad Apps in One Hour for Lawyers
By Tom Mighell

Product Code: 5110739 • **LP Price:** $19.95 • **Regular Price:** $34.95

At last count, there were more than 80,000 apps available for the iPad. Finding the best apps often can be an overwhelming, confusing, and frustrating process. iPad Apps in One Hour for Lawyers provides the "best of the best" apps that are essential for any law practice. In just one hour, you will learn about the apps most worthy of your time and attention. This book will describe how to buy, install, and update iPad apps, and help you:

- Find apps to get organized and improve your productivity
- Create, manage, and store documents on your iPad
- Choose the best apps for your law office, including litigation and billing apps
- Find the best news, reading, and reference apps
- Take your iPad on the road with apps for travelers
- Maximize your social networking power
- Have some fun with game and entertainment apps during your relaxation time

Twitter in One Hour for Lawyers
By Jared Correia

Product Code: 5110746 • **LP Price:** $24.95 • **Regular Price:** $39.95

More lawyers than ever before are using Twitter to network with colleagues, attract clients, market their law firms, and even read the news. But to the uninitiated, Twitter's short messages, or tweets, can seem like they are written in a foreign language. Twitter in One Hour for Lawyers will demystify one of the most important social-media platforms of our time and teach you to tweet like an expert. In just one hour, you will learn to:

- Create a Twitter account and set up your profile
- Read tweets and understand Twitter jargon
- Write tweets—and send them at the appropriate time
- Gain an audience—follow and be followed
- Engage with other Twitters users
- Integrate Twitter into your firm's marketing plan
- Cross-post your tweets with other social media platforms like Facebook and LinkedIn
- Understand the relevant ethics, privacy, and security concerns
- Get the greatest possible return on your Twitter investment
- And much more!

The Lawyer's Essential Guide to Writing
By Marie Buckley

Product Code: 5110726 • **LP Price:** $47.95 • **Regular Price:** $79.95

This is a readable, concrete guide to contemporary legal writing. Based on Marie Buckley's years of experience coaching lawyers, this book provides a systematic approach to all forms of written communication, from memoranda and briefs to e-mail and blogs. The book sets forth three principles for powerful writing and shows how to apply those principles to develop a clean and confident style.

iPad in One Hour for Lawyers, Second Edition
By Tom Mighell

Product Code: 5110747 • **LP Price:** $24.95 • **Regular Price:** $39.95

Whether you are a new or a more advanced iPad user, *iPad in One Hour for Lawyers* takes a great deal of the mystery and confusion out of using your iPad. Ideal for lawyers who want to get up to speed swiftly, this book presents the essentials so you don't get bogged down in technical jargon and extraneous features and apps. In just six, short lessons, you'll learn how to:

- Quickly Navigate and Use the iPad User Interface
- Set Up Mail, Calendar, and Contacts
- Create and Use Folders to Multitask and Manage Apps
- Add Files to Your iPad, and Sync Them
- View and Manage Pleadings, Case Law, Contracts, and other Legal Documents
- Use Your iPad to Take Notes and Create Documents
- Use Legal-Specific Apps at Trial or in Doing Research

30-DAY RISK-FREE ORDER FORM

ABA**LAW**
PRACTICE
DIVISION
The Business of Practicing Law

Please print or type. To ship UPS, we must have your street address.
If you list a P.O. Box, we will ship by U.S. Mail.

Name

Member ID

Firm/Organization

Street Address

City/State/Zip

Area Code/Phone (In case we have a question about your order)

E-mail

Method of Payment:
☐ Check enclosed, payable to American Bar Association
☐ MasterCard   ☐ Visa   ☐ American Express

Card Number   Expiration Date

Signature Required

MAIL THIS FORM TO:
American Bar Association, Publication Orders
P.O. Box 10892, Chicago, IL 60610

ORDER BY PHONE:
24 hours a day, 7 days a week:
Call 1-800-285-2221 to place a credit card
order. We accept Visa, MasterCard, and
American Express.

EMAIL ORDERS: orders@americanbar.org
FAX ORDERS: 1-312-988-5568

VISIT OUR WEB SITE: www.ShopABA.org
Allow 7-10 days for regular UPS delivery. Need it
sooner? Ask about our overnight delivery options.
Call the ABA Service Center at 1-800-285-2221
for more information.

GUARANTEE:
If—for any reason—you are not satisfied with your
purchase, you may return it within 30 days of
receipt for a refund of the price of the book(s).
No questions asked.

Thank You For Your Order.

Join the ABA Law Practice Division today and receive a substantial discount on Division publications!

Product Code:	Description:	Quantity:	Price:	Total Price:
				$
				$
				$
				$
				$

Shipping/Handling:				
$0.00 to $9.99	add $0.00		Subtotal:	$
$10.00 to $49.99	add $6.95	*Tax: IL residents add 9.25% DC residents add 6%	*Tax:	$
$50.00 to $99.99	add $8.95		**Shipping/Handling:	$
$100.00 to $199.99	add $10.95	Yes, I am an ABA member and would like to join the Law Practice Division today! (Add $50.00)		$
$200.00 to $499.99	add $13.95		Total:	$